Materials and Concepts in Jazz Improvisation

A Theory of Jazz Improvisation for Beginning and Advanced Players

Kurt Ellenberger, D.M.A.

Keytone • Grand Rapids • 2005
www.assayer.org

Fifth Edition

Printed in the United States of America

ISBN 0-9709811-3-9

A Keytone Publication • Grand Rapids, MI

Book design by Dan Royer

For my students . . .

Contents

PART THREE: ADVANCED CONCEPTS IN HARMONY AND VOICE-LEADING

Preface

"There is no denying that to learn a new system takes time and trouble. But if one gains both a wider outlook and a more complete mastery, it is worth it. Technical skill can never be great enough. No one is too able or too accomplished to learn more than he knows. Technique must be learned as a child learns to move his limbs; what was difficult at first must become easy; it must be at one's instantaneous disposal; it must function so perfectly that its action is no longer noticed; it must sink to the level of subconscious activity." (Hindemith 11)

So writes Paul Hindemith in the introductory first chapter of his important pedagogical series entitled *The Craft of Musical Composition*. These words (from the pen of one of this century's greatest composers and most philosophically sound musical thinkers) are applicable not only to music or music composition or even art in general, but to all manner of human activity, especially those requiring large-scale integration of conceptual information. The oft overlooked part of this discussion is contained within the last sentence of the Hindemith quote: *it must sink to the level of subconscious activity*. When we see the performance of a master (whether it be a master pianist, a master improviser, or a master tennis player) we see only the effortless command of the materials involved, the apparent display of what appears to be a pre-ordained talent or skill.

What is not immediately apparent—the extreme self-discipline, the years and years of arduous and backbreaking intellectual or physical labor, the intense study, the energy of a lifetime focused on a single task- is precisely what makes the former activity possible. (This is not to be confused with a pedantic glorification of technique—as if it had some intrinsic value *outside* of its end goal.) This deception is even greater when the music is seemingly simple: Bill Evans' "simple" improvisation in *My Man's Gone Now*, or the "simple" melody in Ravel's *Pavane for a Dead Princess*, or the "simple" chord progression upon which Bach's *Goldberg Variations* are based; all are examples of this deception. The many years of struggle and study that provide the creator with a solid foundation are hidden from immediate view, but are what allows the artist to be simple, without being simplistic. There is indeed a great difference between the two. The true master can speak volumes with only a few well-chosen notes, however, the price paid for those few precious notes (for learning which notes to choose) is extremely high.

However, when technique is mastered to such a point that it becomes subconscious, it then also becomes seemingly effortless; artistic expression is then allowed to flourish unabated by mere technical concerns. It is important for the beginner and professional alike to be aware of this deception; for the beginner so that they realize what lies ahead; for the professional so that they remember their own journey, thereby constructing a sound pedagogy which is sympathetic to the beginner's precarious and difficult situation.

It is for the serious student that this text is then intended. It contains the information needed to successfully approach the vast majority of jazz literature, both past and present. It is not a workbook of exercises and studies. There are already many texts commercially available that provide countless thousands of patterns, exercises, and the like.[1] This text differs in that it presents the information using language appropriate to the depth of the subject matter, something I believe is lacking in the world of jazz. My purpose here is to address the problems faced by the improviser in a manner that is logical, concise, and above all conceptual in nature. Today's jazz musician must have the ability to deal in an extemporaneous fashion with all the melodic and harmonic devices found in the history of music— from the modal language of the Medieval and Renaissance eras through the complicated and often abstract music of Shostakovich, Hindemith, Bartok, Stravinsky, Debussy and others. Thus, jazz is inextricably tied to western music and its canon, making it necessary (and more efficient) to address its pedagogy using the existing terminology of music theory (a discipline which has been describing these devices in their classical context decades before they were employed by jazz musicians) (Lees, 218-19). I hope that this text will provide you with the information and approach necessary to succeed in this endeavor.

Finally, I would like to acknowledge with special thanks, my wife, Rebecca, for all the countless hours of editorial work and artistic guidance, to say nothing of the support and enouragment that allowed me to undertake the project in the first place. And to Dan Royer for his kind assistance and wise counsel in the design and development of the book, which was, as always, far beyond the call of duty.

To the Student

When you begin to teach jazz, the most dangerous thing is that you tend to teach style . . . I had eleven piano students, and I would say eight of them didn't even want to know anything about chords or anything—they didn't want to do anything that anybody had ever done, because they didn't want to be imitators. Well, of course, this is pretty naive. . . but nevertheless it does bring to light the fact that if you're going to try to teach jazz . . . you must abstract the principles of music which have nothing to do with style, and this is exceedingly difficult. . . It ends up where the jazz player, ultimately, if he's going to be a serious jazz player, teaches himself. Bill Evans (Pettinger 89)

The purpose of this text is to provide the student with a reference that contains all of the most important concepts (primarily harmonic and melodic concepts) found in jazz improvisation. Some exercises have been provided, however these are very limited in nature. In an attempt to remain true to Evans' ideal as stated above, I have tried to do this in a manner that does not impose style, but rather elucidates musical principles that are the same in jazz as they are in classical music.

This text assumes that the student has a certain minimum amount of facility on their instrument which includes the ability to:

i) play all major and minor scales over the entire range of the instrument, *and*

ii) arpeggiate all major, minor, and diminished triads and chords of all types over the entire range of the instrument.

Students are also expected to be reasonably familiar with rudimentary concepts of music theory such as key signatures, time signatures, intervals, construction of major, minor, and diminished triads, and seventh chords of all types. Some students will be somewhat prepared in terms of instrumental technique, while many will likely be unprepared for the theory component. For those who fall into this category, I suggest purchasing a copy of *Elementary Rudiments of Music* by Barbara Wharram (published by Frederick Harris Music and available at most music stores) for some remedial work in this vital area.

As mentioned in the preface, this text does not contain many exercises and/or patterns. It is assumed that much of this type of information is obvious—scales and patterns should be practiced as follows:

i) in all keys (if key-related),

ii) starting on any pitch (if not key-related),

iii) in every conceivable numerical pattern (thirds, fourths, fifths; ascending and descending),

iv) using a variety of rhythmic patterns,

v) over the entire range of the instrument played, and

vi) in an experimental and creative manner—the onus is on you to be creative in all aspects involved in this pursuit.

I trust that the book's terminology and descriptions are accessible, perhaps with the help of a teacher, for most students. Do note, however, that numbers with carets above them refer to scale degrees. Thus, $\hat{1}$ is to be read as "scale degree one."

Be diligent, consistent, and disciplined—the task is difficult but not impossible. As with all things, success comes to those who are focused and committed, not necessarily those who have precocious, natural talent.

—Kurt Ellenberger

Chapter 1: Keyboard Techniques for the Non-Pianist

Improvisation presents an immense challenge to a musician. The reason for this is simple: the task requires that the improviser understand all elements of music, (most importantly, melody, harmony, and rhythm) to a degree such that they are able to literally compose at will within a tonal or neo-tonal environment. As such, it is essential for all instrumentalists to acquire some rudimentary piano skills, in order to understand that element which is often mysterious and elusive to monophonic instrumentalists—the element of harmony. The following exercises are designed for non-pianists[2] and beginning jazz pianists to help them acquire rudimentary skills in jazz harmony.

1.1 Keyboard Exercise #1: Diatonic Seventh Chords

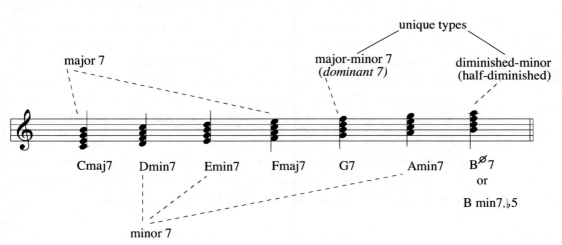

Figure 1

The example above (Figure 1) shows all of the diatonic seventh chords in the key of C major. Note the type of chord found on each scale degree. This pattern will be the same in all keys.

Figure 2 shows all diatonic seventh chords in every major key.

This set of 84 chords contains an enormous amount of information regarding keys, chords, and the relationship between chords and scales. Since jazz is largely *tonal* music, we find a large portion of the standard repertoire comprised of various arrangements of this set of diatonic chords. Familiarity with these chords will provide a strong foundation for the study of harmony and improvisation.

1.2 Keyboard Exercise #2: Diatonic Quartal Sonorities

Jazz harmony features chords built using thirds (called tertian harmony) and, as below, chords built using fourths (both perfect and diminished) which is called quartal harmony. Other types are also used, such as quintal (built using fifths) or secondal (built using seconds) but these are more rare and difficult to categorize for reasons beyond the scope of this discussion.[3] The following exercise will help provide familiarity with the general sound and construction of quartal harmony.

1.3 Keyboard Exercise #3: II-V-I Patterns

The ii-V-I pattern is found everywhere in jazz harmony (as in pieces from tonal music). All jazz instrumentalists need to become intimately familiar with this pattern and its voice-leading. The patterns in the various parts of Figure 3 (consecutive keys in descending whole tone, descending semitone, and ascending minor thirds) are commonly found across eras in jazz.

Play all of these progressions on the piano and memorize them. As you play them, note the voice-leading pattern found in the ii-V-I progression. The chord progression is quite simple if one takes this pattern into account.

Play figures 1, 2 and 3 on the piano and memorize them. In particular, note the voice-leading pattern found in the ii-V-I progression. The chord progression is quite simple if one takes the pattern in figure 4 into account.

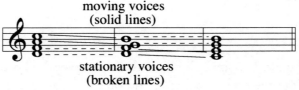

moving voices
(solid lines)

stationary voices
(broken lines)

Figure 4

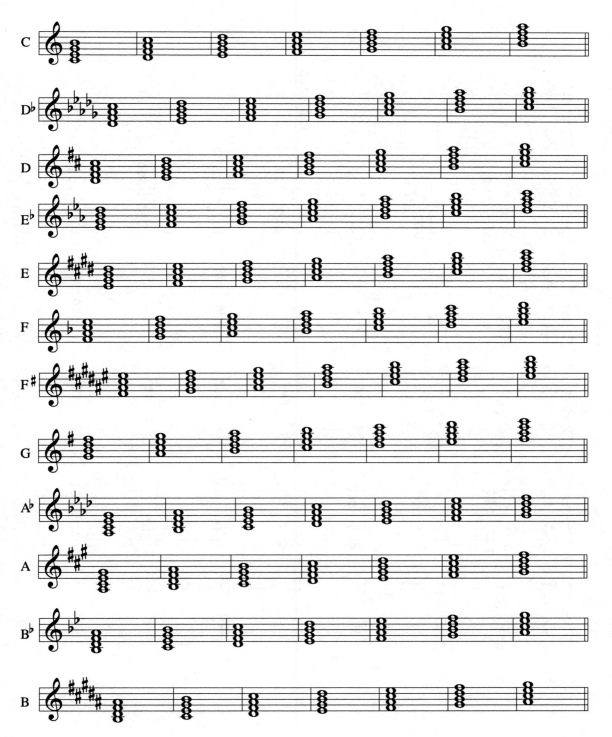

Figure1 in all 12 keys

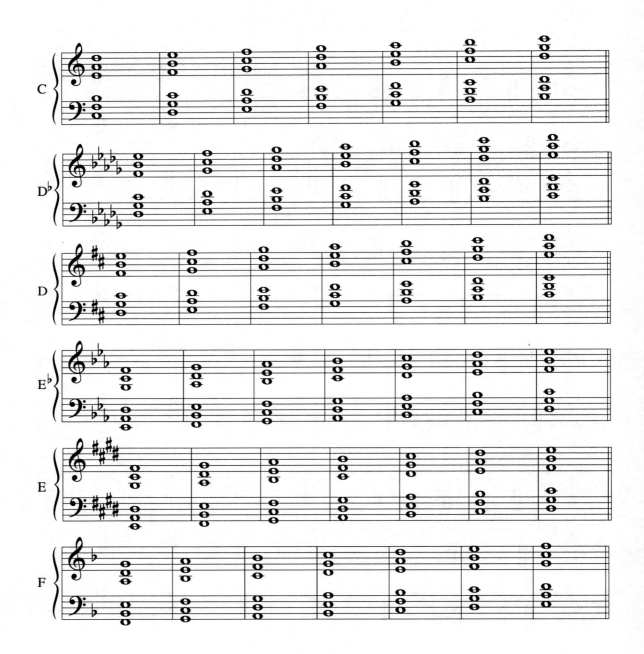

Figure 2

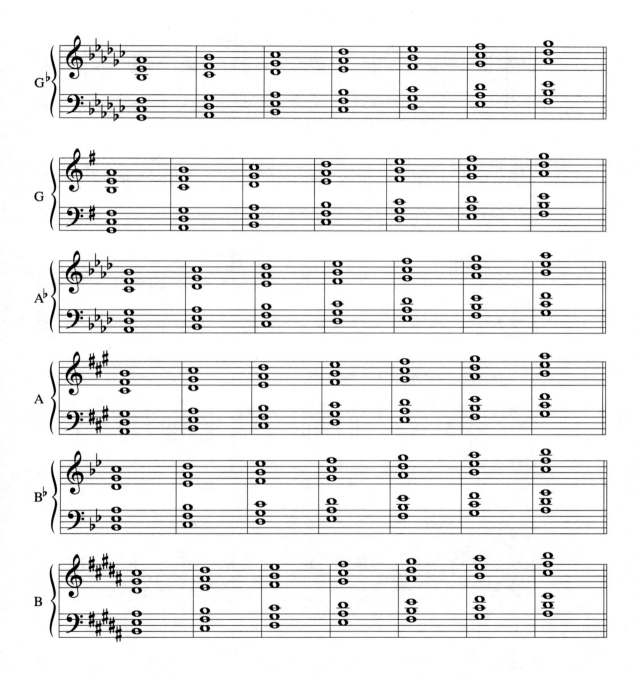

Figure 2 cont.

a) ii-V-I in Descending Whole Tone Pattern (Part 1)

b) ii-V-I in Descending Whole Tone Pattern (Part 2)

Figure 3

c) ii-V-I in Descending Semitone Pattern

Figure 3 cont.

d) ii-V-I in Ascending Minor Thirds

Figure 3 cont.

Chapter 2: A Polychordal Approach to Upper Structure Harmonies

Jazz harmony relies heavily on tertian harmony, as previously stated. Instead of stopping at the seventh of each chord as the highest numbered pitch, jazz harmony almost always uses chords with sevenths, ninths, elevenths, and thirteenths.[4] These upper structure additions can also be altered by raising or lowering them by a half-step. The result is a very large number of variations (some subtly varied, others drastically varied) of a relatively small number of four-note chords.

Now we will build a common jazz chord-C7, 9, #11, 13—using only the information provided by chord symbol.

The first two characters tell us that the chord is C7—meaning that it is a major-minor seventh, or in other words, a simple dominant seventh chord (found as a diatonic seventh chord the key of F major) with C as its root. See example below:

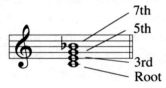

7th
5th
3rd
Root

Figure 5

Now we will add the upper structure as required by the chord symbol. The '9' in the symbol means to add the pitch that is a major ninth above the root of the chord, '#11' means to add the pitch a perfect eleventh above the root of the chord and then *raise* it by one half-step, and finally '13' means to add the pitch a major thirteenth above the root of the chord.

13th
#11th
9th

Figure 6

This is a time-consuming process, especially if one builds these large chords using this step-by-step process. A jazz musician needs to build these types of chords at sight, on any root, quickly and accurately. Often times the alterations are much more complicated than in the example above, and could quickly move to another chord with complicated alterations, and then to another, and so on. Building chords in the manner used above is far too time consuming because it is non-conceptual. Fortunately, there is another way to construct these difficult chords that is more conceptual, and therefore faster and more accurate. This is accomplished by looking at the pitches that make up the *upper structure* and viewing them as a separate layer in the chord in question. Look at the upper structure of the chord in our example—D (ninth), F♯ (raised eleventh), and A (thirteenth). Here they are on a staff:

Figure 7

Obviously, this is simply a D major triad. So, if we look at the original chord as two layers—one layer is a dominant seventh chord on C, and the other is a D major triad—it becomes much easier to build the chord in one step, rather than four or five tedious steps. This process takes into account the fact that two different chords appear to be superimposed—one on top of the other. In reality, these two different chords actually function as part of a tertian structure. However, thinking of them as two separate entities allows for faster, more accurate realization of the required tertian chord. The name given this approach is taken from the phenomenon it describes—a chord which is made up of two different chords is called a polychord.[5] This term is usually and properly applied to chords whose constituent triads cannot be explained as part of a larger tertian chord. For example: a C major triad combined with an F♯ major triad (the so-called Petrushka Chord from Stravinsky's ballet of the same name) is a legitimate polychord. The example above is not a true polychord because it is a tertian chord in both function and construction. Thus, I call this the polychordal approach to learning upper structure harmony. Admittedly, this approach still involves some calculation, but it is a process which, in time, allows for these structures and sounds to become internalized to the point of being virtually automatic. This is the manner in which most jazz musicians conceptualize these complicated structures. Let us now see how this process functions in practice:

Here are ten of the most common chords found in jazz (for the sake of example, all have C as their root):

1. Cmajor7, 9, #11, 13
2. C7, 9, #11, 13
3. C7, ♭9, 13
4. C7, ♭9, #11
5. C7, ♭9, ♭13
6. C7, ♭9, #11, 13
7. C7, #9
8. C7, #9, #11
9. C7, #9, ♭13[6]
10. C min7, ♭5, 9, 11

Imagine for a moment how difficult it would be to spell just these ten examples using the tedious note-by-note process. Fortunately, there is a more efficient and reliable way. If we relate the roots and chord types of the two layers, we can spell these chords much faster than the other method.

In order to demonstrate this method, we will use chord #1, (C major 7, 9, #11, 13), (which we now know is a simple D major triad superimposed on top of a C major 7 chord) in the following example. The roots of these two chords are one whole step apart—the root of the upper structure triad (D) is the pitch that is one whole step above the root of the base chord (C). The base chord is a major seventh type, while the upper structure is a simple major triad.[7] Thus, we can spell chord #1 easily if we generalize this process in the following manner:

1. To spell any chord 'X major 7, 9, #11, 13' (with X as any possible root), build a major triad on the pitch one whole step up from X, and place that triad on top of "X major 7.

Figure 8

This process can be repeated quickly using any root, if one remembers the formula above. Thus, to spell "Dmaj7, 9, #11, 13" one need only build a major triad on the pitch one whole step above the root of the base chord, superimpose it on top of the base chord, and one will have correctly spelled the required sonority. Perform this operation and build this chord in your mind before reading on. You should be visualizing an E major triad on top of a D major seventh chord, which contains all of the required pitches.

At first, this may seem equally as time-consuming and tedious as the other method. But, with this polychordal approach, one only need memorize a few dozen of these formulae, rather than memorizing thousands and thousands of different chords—all of which must be at the fingertips of every professional jazz musician. When viewed in this light, it should be obvious that the polychordal approach is an indispensable conceptual tool. It is absolutely necessary for every aspiring jazz musician to learn these simple formulae.

Now, we will do the same for the remaining nine chords from our list of commonly found jazz chords.

2. C7, 9, ♯11, 13

To spell X 7, 9, ♯11, 13 build a *major triad* on the pitch a *major second up* from the root of the base chord. Thus for C7, 9, ♯11, 13, place a D major triad on top of C7.

Figure 9

3. C7, ♭9, 13

To spell X 7, ♭9, 13 build a *major triad* on the pitch a *major sixth up* from the root of the base chord. Thus, for C7, ♭9, 13 place an A major triad on top of C7.

Figure 10

4. C7, ♭9, ♯11

To spell X 7, ♭9, ♯11 build a *major triad* on the pitch an *augmented fourth or diminished fifth up* from the root of the base chord. Thus, for C7, ♭9, ♯11, place an F♯/G♭ major triad on top of C7.

Figure 11

5. C7, ♭9, ♭13

To spell X 7, ♭9, ♭13 build a *minor triad* on the pitch a *augmented fourth or diminished fifth up* from the root of the base chord. Thus, for C7, ♭9, ♭13 place an F♯/G♭ minor triad on top of C7.

Figure 12

6. C7, ♭9, ♯11, 13

To spell *X 7, ♭9, ♯11, 13* build a *minor triad* on the pitch a *minor second up* from the root of the base chord. Thus, for C7, ♭9, ♯11, 13 place a D♭ minor triad on top of C7.

Figure 13

7. C7, #9

To spell *X 7, #9* build a *major triad* on the pitch a *minor third up* from the root of the base chord. Thus, for C7, #9 place an E♭ major triad on top of C7.

Figure 14

8. C7, #9, #11

To spell *X 7, #9, #11* build a *minor triad* on the pitch a *minor third up* from the root of the base chord. Thus, for C7, #9, #11 place an E♭ minor triad on top of C7.

Figure 15

9. C7, #9, ♭13

To spell *X 7, #9* build a *major triad* on the pitch a *minor sixth up* from the root of the base chord. Thus, for C7, #9, ♭13 place an A♭ major triad on top of C7.

Figure 16

10. C min 7, ♭5, 9, 11

To spell *X min 7, ♭5, 9, 11* build a *major triad* on the pitch a *minor seventh up* from the root of the base chord. Thus, for C min7, ♭5, 9, 11 place a B♭ major triad on top of Cmin7, ♭5.

Figure 17

This list is by no means complete. There are literally thousands of ways in which two or more chords can be combined in this manner. However, the memorization and careful application of the procedures listed here will provide the performer with a solid foundation for dealing with the complicated tertian structures found in jazz.

In order to achieve a higher level of sophistication in dealing with these upper structure chords, one must take note of and subsequently show respect for the purely linear aspects of their construction. These pseudo-polychordal chords function best when there is good voice-leading between subsequent chords. It is extremely difficult (if not impossible) to define a set of "rules" which can be applied in this endeavor. Music of any kind requires far too much creativity to allow for such dogmatism. That being said, there are three general principles that will, if followed, result in better voicings. They are as follows:

   i) maintain independence of line whenever possible;

   ii) search for contrary motion between voices; and

   iii) use step-wise motion rather than leaps.

In other words, the same concepts involved in the chorale-style writing assignments found in most freshman and sophomore theory courses apply equally well to jazz.[8]

In order to demonstrate this concept, play the following example on the piano:

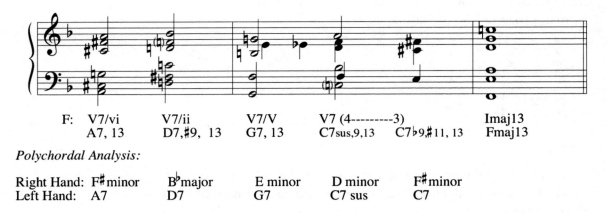

F:	V7/vi	V7/ii	V7/V	V7 (4---------3)		Imaj13
	A7, 13	D7,♯9, 13	G7, 13	C7sus,9,13	C7♭9,♯11, 13	Fmaj13

Polychordal Analysis:

Right Hand:	F♯minor	B♭major	E minor	D minor	F♯minor
Left Hand:	A7	D7	G7	C7 sus	C7

Figure 18

Follow each pitch (especially in the right hand) as it moves *linearly,* and observe the step-wise motion, the relatively independent movement, and the contrary motion between voices. Note also, that enharmonic spellings are used freely. For example, the raised ninth in the D7, ♯9 chord should properly be spelled as E♯, but for the sake of simplicity, it is spelled as its enharmonic equivalent, F♮. The same is true for the lowered ninth in the C7 chord—it should be spelled D♭ but instead, it is spelled as C♯. These enharmonic spellings are used because they make it much easier to visualize the upper structure as a simple major or minor triad.

Chapter 3: Beginning Techniques and Tools of Improvisation

Transcribing solos and entire songs is essential for every jazz musician. There is no better way to acquire proper jazz phrasing. Also, scales and patterns will become meaningful only when placed in proper context—context that can be learned most efficiently by transcribing. Transcription is an intense and musically relevant form of aural skills training, and as such, will also contribute greatly to general musicianship, regardless of context.

3.1 Transcription: Aural Skills for the Jazz Musician

There is no secret to the art of transcribing pitches and rhythms by ear. Begin with clean staff paper, a good pencil or fountain pen, and a clean, smudge-free eraser. Then, find a quiet room and sit down with your instrument and a tape deck or CD player and begin transcribing the solo of your choice. [Note: CD players are preferable because the pitch is much more accurate than the unreliable speed (and therefore pitches) of even the best cassette players.]

Follow these step-by-step guidelines, and you will see incredible improvements in your improvisational skills soon after you begin transcribing:

1. Listen to the solo enough so that it is possible to sing along. This will afford a level of familiarity with the material *prior to transcription* than would otherwise be possible.

2. Determine the key, meter, and starting pitch.

3. Play a short segment of the recording and use your ear to transcribe the pitches with their correct rhythms. Notate what you have just transcribed on your staff paper.[9] If this seems too difficult, shorten the length of the excerpt, until it becomes possible to do, even if you begin by transcribing only one pitch at a time. Your ear and your memory will improve quickly to meet this new challenge. Eventually, you will be able to transcribe complete phrases in one step. At first, however, keep the length of your example short and you will be successful.

4. Double check what you have just transcribed from the recording by playing it on your instrument. (This step will become less necessary as your ear develops.)

5. Continue in this way until you have finished the entire solo.

6. Learn the solo on your instrument and play along with the recording. Your goal is to match *exactly* the subtle nuances of dynamics, color, rhythmic placements, articulations, etc. of the soloist. Again, one of the most difficult tasks for young improvisers is correct jazz phrasing and style. This task is easily accomplished by transcribing solos and emulating the styles found therein.

7. *Transcribe every day!* Set yourself a goal for daily transcription and commit to that goal. Five measures a day will quickly become a large library of transcriptions, yet will only require 10-15 minutes a day.

8. When you come across a melodic phrase or pattern that you find particularly interesting or attractive, learn it in every key (if key-related) or starting on every pitch (if not key-related). This will provide both a technical and intellectual challenge that will improve your jazz vocabulary greatly.

Suggestions:

1. Make your first transcription a simple one. An ideal choice would be a solo by trumpet player Chet Baker because his playing is relatively simple and his note choices are perfect. In general, choose something from your own collection that does not contain any fast runs or angular figures. Be careful to choose something that is legitimately jazz literature—avoid popular so-called "jazz" musicians who are in reality, far-removed from the world of serious jazz.

2. Half-speed cassette players and other devices are commercially available and are of great assistance in transcription. These machines play the recording at exactly half the original speed, which also lowers the pitches by one octave. This makes transcription much easier, especially those incorporating fast runs or fast tempos. This is not needed for beginning improvisers, but it becomes essential as you progress to more difficult and advanced literature.[10]

3. When you encounter difficulty with a fast line, transcribe up to the beginning of the line, and then transcribe *after* the line, starting at the earliest point at which it again becomes possible to hear what is being played. Armed with knowledge of both the beginning and the *destination* of the line, fill in the middle portion using common sense, tonal theory, and the knowledge of what is possible and idiomatic on your instrument.

3.2 Key Areas: An Approach to Improvisation

The question asked more often than any other by beginning improvisers is: "How do I determine which notes to play over these chord progressions?" While pitch choice is certainly not the only problem faced by the improviser, it is a matter of primary importance, especially to the beginner. Here are some chord changes similar to those found in the first eight measures of a favorite jazz standard recorded by many jazz musicians.

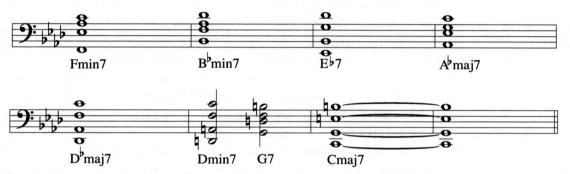

Figure 19

This example was chosen because the key change makes it relatively difficult, especially for the beginner. However, if the example is viewed from the larger perspective of key areas, it becomes relatively simple, even for the beginner.[11] The following is a step-by-step method of determining scale choices that is guaranteed to provide the beginner with the means to successfully begin exploring the harmony of any piece in the standard jazz repertoire.

First, refer back to the work done in section 1.1. (You should have written out all the diatonic seventh chords in every major key.) While there are obvious external differences between all of the keys (key signatures, starting pitches, etc.), these are superficial. There are essential similarities between the keys that are much more important. Since every key is simply a transposition of C major so that it begins and ends on another pitch, all of the relationships between pitches, chords, chord types, etc. in any key are exactly the same as those found in any other key. (This is an important concept—make sure you understand it completely.) Thus, you can check your work from section 1.1 by comparing your results with the example in

C major found on page 3. The only difference between the example given and its transposition to the other keys should be *the roots of the chords*. The chord types and roman numeral analysis should be exactly the same in every key. In other words, every tonic chord (I) should be a major seventh, every super-tonic chord (ii) should be a minor seventh, and so on for every chord. Check to make sure that this is true of your work. Again, this is an important concept, make sure you understand it completely before proceeding.

What does this tell us about the various chord types in each key?[12] It tells us that, logically, most of these 48 chords must exist as diatonic seventh chords in more than one key. This is, in fact, the case. For example, look at the supertonic (ii) chord in C major, which is D minor7. It exists as ii min7 in C major, but it also exists as iii min7 in B♭ major, and yet again as vi min7 in F major. The same will be true of every other minor seventh chord in the key. Now we will look at the subdominant (IV) in C major, which is F maj7. It exists in C major as IV maj7, but also exists as I maj7 in the key of F major. (Check figure 1 to verify.) Do you see a pattern emerging here? The number of times the chord type appears in any key is equal to the number of keys in which that same chord exists as a diatonic seventh chord.

Here is figure 1 from section 1.1 once again:

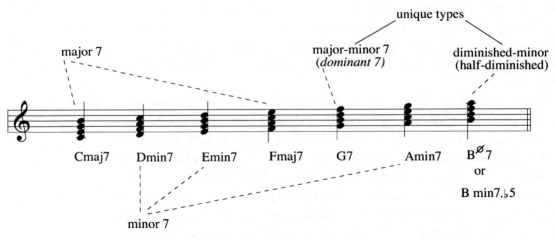

Figure 1

There are three occurrences of the minor seventh chord type (ii, iii, and vi), two occurrences of the major seventh chord type (I and IV), but only one occurrence of the dominant chord type (V) and only one occurrence of the half-diminished chord type (vii). Keeping this phenomenon in mind, it becomes very easy to determine the various keys (or key in the case of the dominant and half-diminished variety) in which any given seventh chord exists as a diatonic seventh chord. The following section outlines the process by which one can determine the keys in which any given chord can be found as a diatonic seventh chord:

1. Every minor 7th chord exists as:

   a) *ii min7* in the major key a major second down from the root of the chord in question,

   b) *iii min7* in the major key a major third down from the root of the chord in question, and

   c) *vi min7* in the major key a major sixth down from the root of the chord in question.

2. Every major 7th chord exists as:

   a) *Imaj7* in the major key starting on the root of the chord in question,

   b) *IVmaj7* in the major key a perfect fourth down from the root of the chord in question.

3. Every dominant seventh chord exists as:

   a) *V7* in the major key a perfect fifth down from the root of the chord in question.

4. Every half-diminished seventh chord exists as:

   a) *vii min 7, ♭5* in the major key a major seventh down (minor second up) from the root of the chord in question.

What does all this have to do with scale choices and improvisation? The process of determining the key(s) in which a certain chord occurs diatonically provides the improviser with invaluable information regarding scale choices which will interact in a pleasing (consonant) manner over the chords in question. Thus, by determining the key(s) in which a certain chord occurs diatonically, the improviser has also determined the major scale(s) that are appropriate for use in conjunction with those chords. Now we will see how this functions as an aid to determining some initial scale choices for the example cited earlier. In order to do this, we will determine the keys in which each of these chords occurs diatonically.

1. Chord in measure 1: Fminor7

This is a minor seventh chord, and as such:

a) it exists as *ii min7* in the major key a major second down from the root of the chord in question.

QUESTION: In which major key does this chord exist as ii min7?

ANSWER: By performing the operation above, we determine that the key is $E\flat$ *major.*

and

b) it exists as *iii min7* in the major key a major third down from the root of the chord in question.

Q: In which major key does this chord exist as iii min7?

A: By performing the operation above, we determine that the key is $D\flat$ *major.*

and

c) it exists as *vi min7* in the major key a major sixth down from the root of the chord in question.

Q: In which major key does this chord exist as vi min7?

A: By performing the operation above, we determine that the key is $A\flat$ *major.*

Verify these results with figure 1b from section 1.1.

2. Chord in measure 2: $B\flat$ minor 7

This is another minor seventh chord, and as such:

a) it exists as *ii min7* in the major key a major second down from the root of the chord in question.

Q: In which major key does this chord exist as ii min7?

A: By performing the operation above, we determine that the key is
A♭ major.

and

b) it exists as *iii min7* in the major key a major third down from the
root of the chord in question.

Q: In which major key does this chord exist as iii min7?

A: By performing the operation above, we determine that the key is
G♭ major.

and

c) it exists as *vi min7* in the major key a major sixth down from the
root of the chord in question.

Q: In which major key does this chord exist as vi min7?

A: By performing the operation above, we determine that the key is
D♭ major.

3. Chord in measure 3: E♭ 7

This is a dominant seventh chord, and as such:

it exists as *V7* in the major key a perfect fifth down from the root of
the chord in question.

Q: In which major key does this chord exist as V7?

A: By performing the operation above, we determine that the key is
A♭ major.

4. Chord in measure 4: A♭ major 7

This is a major seventh chord, and as such:

a) it exists as *Imaj7* in the major key starting on the root of the chord
in question.

Q: In which major key does this chord exist as Imaj7?

A: By performing the operation above, we determine that the key is A♭ *major.*

and

b) it exists as *IVmaj7* in the major key a perfect fourth down from the root of the chord in question.

Q: In which major key does this chord exist as IVmaj7?

A: By performing the operation above, we determine that the key is E♭ *major.*

5. Chord in measure 5: D♭ major 7

This is a major seventh chord, and as such:

a) it exists as *Imaj7* in the major key starting on the root of the chord in question.

Q: In which major key does this chord exist as Imaj7?

A: By performing the operation above, we determine that the key is D♭ *major.*

and

b) it exists as *IVmaj7* in the major key a perfect fourth down from the root of the chord in question.

Q: In which major key does this chord exist as IVmaj7?

A: By performing the operation above, we determine that the key is A♭ *major.*

6. Chord in measure 6, beats 1 and 2: D minor 7

This is another minor seventh chord, and as such:

a) it exists as *ii min7* in the major key a major second down from the root of the chord in question.

Q: In which major key does this chord exist as ii min7?

A: By performing the operation above, we determine that the key is *C major.*

and

b) it exists as *iii min 7* in the major key a major third down from the root of the chord in question.

Q: In which major key does this chord exist as iii min7?

A: By performing the operation above, we determine that the key is *B♭ major.*

and

c) it exists as *vi min7* in the major key a major sixth down from the root of the chord in question.

Q: In which major key does this chord exist as vi min7?

A: By performing the operation above, we determine that the key is *F major.*

7. Chord in measure 6, beats 3 and 4: G7

This is a dominant seventh chord, and as such:

it exists as *V7* in the major key a perfect fifth down from the root of the chord in question.

Q: In which major key does this chord exist as V7?

A: By performing the operation above, we determine that the key is *C major.*

8. Chord in measures 7 and 8: C major 7

This is a major seventh chord, and as such:

a) it exists as *Imaj7* in the major key starting on the root of the chord in question.

Q: In which major key does this chord exist as Imaj7?

A: By performing the operation above, we determine that the key is *C major.*

and

b) it exists as *IVmaj7* in the major key a perfect fourth down from the root of the chord in question.

Q: In which major key does this chord exist as IVmaj7?

A: By performing the operation above, we determine that the key is *G major.*

What does this information tell us about possible scale choices in this eight measure example? We can summarize all of this information regarding keys as follows:

E♭: ii min7   A♭: ii min7   A♭: V7   A♭: I maj7
D♭: iii min7   G♭: iii min7   E♭: IVmaj7
A♭: vi min7   D♭: vi min7

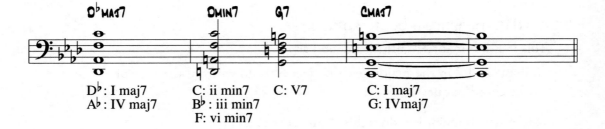

D♭: I maj7   C: ii min7   C: V7   C: I maj7
A♭: IV maj7   B♭: iii min7   G: IVmaj7
                F: vi min7

Figure 20

Notice that the diagram bears out our earlier findings—namely that:
a) under each minor seventh chord, one finds *three* different keys,
b) under each major seventh chord, one finds *two* different keys,
c) under each dominant seventh chord, one finds only one key.[13]

The final step in this process involves a careful analysis of the key areas with the goal of *finding the least possible number of key areas which also contain the highest possible number of consecutive chords* . So, we will now repeat the example above, with one difference—this time, we will isolate the key areas in accordance with the principle stated above. Here is the example once again:

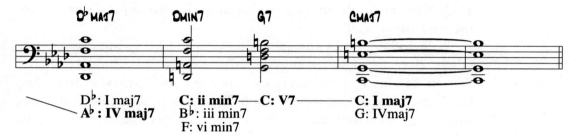

Figure 21

Note that (while there are several different keys in which most of the chords occur diatonically) the chords in the first five measures have one key in common—namely A♭ major (highlighted). Thus, the A♭ major scale will work very well with all of the chords in the first five measures—making it an excellent choice, especially for the beginner. Then, in measure six, there is a key change to C major. All of the chords in the last three measures also have one key in common—namely C major. Thus, the C major scale is the best choice for the last three measures of the example.

Now, we will simplify all of this information and then look at the example from a distance—a "bird's eye view" if you will:

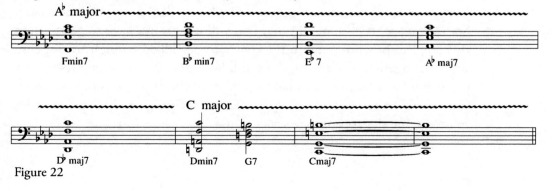

Figure 22

In doing so, we have now simplified the task immensely. Instead of eight, separate, unrelated entities (chords), we now have only two entities (in this case, two different key areas)[14] with which to concern ourselves. In other words, with this new information in hand, we need only be concerned with two major scales (with which we are all, hopefully, very familiar) and the point at which the key change occurs. This approach will work with the vast majority of jazz standards.

Seven Frequently Asked Questions

1. Q: What about the other keys that most of these chords exist in? Are they not also useful?

A: The other keys can be used as well but some may work better than others, given the right circumstance. These other keys introduce pitches that can be somewhat foreign to the actual key area, thereby often adding interesting color to the improvisation. This leads to the concept of *modes* which is a more advanced concept in improvisation (discussed in section 1.3.6).

2. Q: It seems to me that this is too much work. Do I have to do this with every single piece I learn?

A: Yes and no. Yes, it is a lot of work, and yes, you will have to do the same thing for every piece. But, you will quickly learn that every piece (in the standard repertoire) is made up of a different combination of the same 48 chords (12 pitches x 4 chord types=48 different chords).[15] Thus, once you've worked through a few different pieces, you'll begin to see chords that you've seen before, in combinations that you have also seen before. The process then begins to speed up considerably, until (in time) it becomes automatic—meaning that you will be able to determine scale choices at sight.. You will also begin to see other patterns that occur as staples in most tonal music, the recognition of which will also become automatic. So, the answer is also 'no,' in that you will not always have to go through this lengthy process—only until you become skilled enough to dispense with it altogether. Even then, there will be times when you are presented a piece that has a particularly challenging set of chord progressions, at which time it will be to your advantage to analyze the piece in this way, in order to determine the appropriate scales to use.

3. Q: I've tried this approach, and the improvisation I come up with sounds odd—it fits with the chords sometimes, and other times it doesn't. Why?

A: This initial approach is somewhat "blunt" in nature—meaning that the scales do not match or outline *any* of the chords in a terribly exacting way, but, they do match *all* of the chords to *some* degree. In other words, the resultant improvisation won't sound *wrong*, but it will also not sound perfectly *right* either. It is a starting point, however. As you become more skilled (through transcription and practice), you will be able to improvise using materials that more closely outline and imply each individual chord (and the linear movements hidden in the chords) and the improvisation will become more intelligent. The materials discussed in the remainder of this text are all ways (generally) in which to make the improvisation more and more specific, more and more tailored to the chord changes, and thus more and more intelligent.

4. Q: I hate music theory! I have always been told that jazz is supposed to be fun, not serious or intellectual. This approach seems to stress a lot of music theory—isn't there a way to do this without having to think about music theory?

A: First of all, if you really hate music theory, you probably won't be very successful as a jazz musician. In fact, the best jazz musicians have studied music theory and classical music (especially from a compositional perspective) very seriously. Here are a few examples:

i) Charlie Parker was fascinated with the music of Prokofiev, Stravinsky and the French Impressionists—he is said to have tried desperately to meet Stravinsky because he recognized in him a kindred musical spirit. He also wanted to study music with the influential French composer, Edgar Varèse, (Lees 213) but unfortunately, did not live to meet or study with either of these two twentieth-century luminaries.

ii) John Coltrane's study of classical music and music theory (Gridley 256) led to his incorporation of chromatic mediant harmonies, harmonies that in large part define his mature compositional style.

iii) Bill Evans was well-steeped in classical music (both from a pianistic and compositional aspect) and music theory, having studied the music and writings of Arnold Schoenberg, (Reilly 24) as well as the music of Ravel, Debussy, Stravinsky, (Reilly 18) Scriabin, J.S. Bach and many others. Evans' sight-reading skills are almost legendary in jazz circles—he sight-read the full instrumental score of Stravinsky's Rite of Spring at the piano, at tempo (!) reportedly without missing a note (Reilly 20). He played a great deal of classical music throughout his life and included sight-reading as an important part of his daily practice regime. As a student at Southeastern Louisiana College, his graduation recital included the Prelude and Fugue in B♭ minor (from J. S. Bach's Well-Tempered Clavier, Book I), Brahms' Capriccio, op. 116, no. 7, Chopin's Scherzo in B♭ minor, and the first movement of Beethoven's Piano Concerto No. 3 (Pettinger 16).

iv) Herbie Hancock was a classical pianist (a genuine child prodigy) before becoming a jazz musician. As a child, he performed Mozart with the Chicago Symphony. The influence of the classical masters and their highly conceptualized innovations (especially twentieth-century masters like Hindemith, Bartok, and Stravinsky) is omnipresent in his playing (Gridley 309).

v) Dave Brubeck was a student of Darius Milhaud. Milhaud thought very highly of Brubeck and actively encouraged him to study counterpoint and composition in order to further develop his improvisatory skills (Lees 49).

vi) Miles Davis' comments from his autobiography speak to this issue:

I took some lessons in symphonic trumpet playing. Trumpet players from the New York Philharmonic gave the lessons, so I learned some things for them. . . Another thing I found strange about living and playing in New York was that a lot of black musicians didn't know anything about music theory . . . A lot of the old guys thought that. . . if you learned something from theory, then [you] would lose the feeling in your playing. . . I would go to the library and borrow scores by all those great composers, like Stravinsky, Alban Berg, Prokofiev. I wanted to see what was going on in all of music. Knowledge is freedom and ignorance is slavery, and I just couldn't believe someone could be that close to freedom and not take advantage of it. (Davis 60, 74)

vii) Rick Margitza, one of the most exciting new voices in jazz tenor saxophone (who was discovered by Miles Davis in the early 1980's) took two years off at a point in his career when most would be working feverishly to establish themselves as a permanent voice in the jazz community. He felt that his time would be better spent studying classical composition, rather than performing. During that time, he wrote two symphonies.[16]

viii) And finally, Gene Lees provides a short list of musicians who showed a great deal of interest in classical music and its ideas:

Coleman Hawkins had a great taste for classical music and was known to haunt museums, particularly art galleries, and many of the founding pianists in jazz, including Willie "the Lion" Smith, James P. Johnson, Fats Waller, Earl Hines, and particularly Teddy Wilson, had considerable knowledge of the classical piano literature. Sidney Bechet was a great lover of Beethoven. Don Redman had two conservatory degrees . . . the extent to which many significant founding figures in jazz had solid academic credentials, including Jimmie Lunceford, who had a bachelor's degree in music and taught the subject [has been well documented]. (Lees 213-14)

This list could continue in this manner for many pages. The connections between jazz musicians, classical music, and music theory are far too numerous to catalogue. Jazz musicians are vitally interested in the "how" and "why" of music. Since this is the realm of music theory, they have availed themselves of its study, in order to acquire knowledge indispensable to the improviser, regardless of genre. (Remember, that many of the most important classical masters like Bach, Mozart, Beethoven, Chopin, Scriabin, and Ravel, to name a few, were also fantastic improvisers.) In short, a jazz musician who is not interested in the "how" and "why" of music is virtually a contradiction in terms.

5. Q: Why can't I just play through this piece and let my ear figure out what pitches I should play rather than doing all of these theory exercises?

A: You can do just that, if you wish. The disadvantage is that you will have to approach each new piece *as a new piece*, instead of building a musical "vocabulary" made up of the many devices (both melodic and harmonic) found in tonal music. The other method (while initially more time-consuming) allows for an accumulation of knowledge that soon begins to outpace the less-conceptual method.

6. Q: I've never seen any professional jazz musicians doing this—is it really done this way?

A: Yes. The reason you have not seen professionals doing this is that they have reached a level where they perform this process instantaneously. On the other hand, when the music is especially difficult, or new, professionals of the highest order will perform this type of analysis in order to shorten the learning process and also to ensure a high level of familiarity with the material. I witnessed this myself when I played with Kenny Wheeler in 1992. When presented with new pieces of improvisatory music, he studied the chord changes and wrote out two or three possible scale choices over top of each chord. His intellectual approach resulted in an almost immediate mastery of the extremely difficult material (mostly circumpolar chords[17]). I was impressed with the fact that, if someone of Wheeler's stature is not beyond the mundane task of writing scale choices over the top of the chord symbols, then it must certainly be appropriate for us lesser mortals to avail ourselves of this tool, without any shame or uneasiness.

7. Q: What about creativity and expression? Doesn't all of this technical talk negate the creative and intuitive aspects of jazz?

A: To be sure, creativity and expression are of paramount importance in the realm of artistic endeavors. However, in order to be creative and expressive, one must first have something that one wants to create, and, in order to bring this creation into the world, one must have a means by which to create it. The more knowledge and skill one has in regards to the means of expression, the greater the probability that one's artistic expression will be profound, lasting, and meaningful. If intellectual innocence and naiveté actually did result in art of greater depth, meaning, and originality (as the popular bromide states), then the most creative among us would be those under the age of two—or better yet, one! Imagine the same discussion in regards to one of the other arts: "Hemingway is my favorite author, and I've decided that I want to be a writer and write one of the great novels of our time. But, I don't want to ruin the more intuitive, innocent, and creative side of my nature, so I'm not going to learn about grammar, spelling, syntax, plot, character development, style, dramatic conflict, or anything else of a technical nature that might spoil my creativity.[18] And, please don't ask me to read or study any of the great works of literature—I wish to remain blissfully unaware of anything that has been done before, so as not to be influenced by it."[19] Of course, this stance would be ridiculous. In short, creativity does not exist in a void.

Knowledge is the opposite of a hindrance in this pursuit, it is an essential means to success in this difficult undertaking.[20] Those who wish to avoid knowledge in order to cultivate "freedom" might enjoy Dizzy Gillespie's comments on a certain "free" tenor saxophonist who ". . . was the original freedom player. Freedom from melody, freedom from harmony, and freedom from time"(Lees 219). Needless to say, this unfortunate saxophonist was not very welcome on Gillespie's stage.

3.3 The Be-Bop Scales

The be-bop scales[21] are staples of jazz improvisation. Each scale converts the seven-note major scale into an eight-note scale by placing a passing tone between $\hat{5}$ and $\hat{6}$ (be-bop #1) or between $\hat{4}$ and $\hat{5}$ (be-bop #2).[22] These scales allow for more congruence between meter and scale—the most common meter in jazz is 4/4, which has eight eighth notes per measure. The eight-note be-bop scales fit this meter much better than does the seven-note major scale. These two scales also feature a chromatic half-step approach to $\hat{5}$. This tends to emphasize the dominant in a more colorful manner, which in turn helps reinforce the tonic. This is why they are used more often than some of the other types available using the same method.[23] The two scales are notated below in C major (as they might appear over chord changes in the key of C major):

Bebop #1 "Tonic Bebop"[24]

Figure 23

Bebop #2 "Dominant Bebop"

C major

Figure 24

Both be-bop scales should be learned in all major keys. Mastery of these scales will provide the performer with a strong foundation upon which to begin the study of improvisation. As such, these scales are extremely useful tools for the improviser. They can be used successfully over a surprisingly large number of chords and harmonies, as well as virtually every genre in jazz.

Application of Be-Bop Scales

Both be-bop scales are also rather "blunt" tools. These scales are, in varying degree, consonant with all of the diatonic seventh chords in their home key. They can thus be used over any of the diatonic seventh chords in their home key. However, they probably function best over the now-familiar ii-V-I progression. Play the following on the piano:

Bebop 1: *"Tonic" Bebop Scale*

Bebop 2: *"Dominant" Bebop Scale*

Figure 25

Notice the extent to which both scales are consonant with *all* the chords. The scales do not outline any particular *chord*, rather they invoke a particular key area instead. This ability makes it impossible to outline a set of rules to use with these scales. The student should learn these scales until they are "second nature," and then experiment with them over various progressions in order to become personally acquainted with the manner in which they are applied in jazz improvisation.

3.4 Arpeggiation of Related Chords

If you have been listening to jazz improvisers, you will have noticed their remarkable ability to actually *sound* the chord changes within the homophonic line being improvised. Jazz musicians refer to this as "making the [chord] changes." It occurs when the single-note line outlines the important notes within each chord in a linearly intelligent manner, thereby giving the illusion that the entire chord has been played by a series of carefully chosen pitches. One of the ways this is accomplished is by simple arpeggiation of the chords as found on the lead sheet. Now we will simply arpeggiate the chords in the ii-V-I pattern from the key of C major.

Here are two examples of simple arpeggiation of the ii-V-I pattern using quarter notes only:

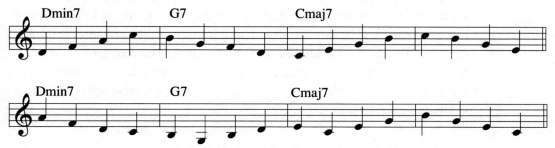

Figure 26

Note that the underlying chords can be heard perfectly well from this single note line, by itself, without the aid of any accompaniment.

Here are two variations that are technically more challenging in which the chords are arpeggiated through their various inversions:

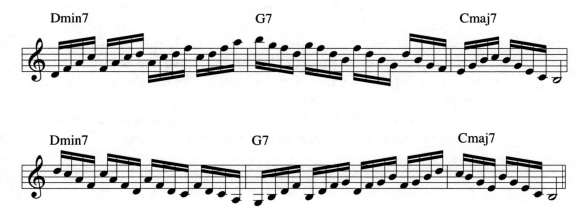

Figure 27

Here is a more difficult arpeggiation that is more angular:

Figure 28

How to Practice Arpeggiation of Related Chords

This is an extremely efficient way to learn new pieces for improvisation. All of the chord changes in a piece should be approached in this manner. From this type of study, the student will acquire a working knowledge of not only the chords, but rather the much more important internal linear motion that creates the chords in the first place. The resultant improvisation will show genuine understanding of the harmonic framework of the piece, and will provide the foundation necessary for advancement in this challenging undertaking.

3.5 Tension and Release: Changing Tones

The improvisatory techniques discussed so far have been, for the most part, fairly consonant. All music aspiring to be labeled "art" must have dramatic conflict of some type. One of the ways this is accomplished in music is through the intelligent use of dissonance. Globally, this may be expressed in the key relationships between different sections of the piece, as in sonata form.[25] Locally, this may be expressed in the use of pitches which are not consonant with the chords over which they appear. One of the structured ways in which jazz musicians learn to create this dissonance locally is through the use of changing tone figures. These figures feature pitches which are mildly to extremely dissonant with the chords over which they are played, thereby creating much-needed musical tension. This tension is then immediately released (dissonance is immediately resolved) as the dissonant pitches move in a step-wise manner into a consonance.[26]

The examples below feature changing tones which surround the chord tones in a ii-V-I progression in C major.

1. Mildly dissonant

Figure 29

The three examples vary dramatically in their dissonance levels. What causes this? The first example uses changing tones that are diatonic to the key resulting in an approach (to the note of resolution) that consists largely of whole-steps. The second example uses some chromatically altered pitches that are not diatonic, making for a more equal blend of half-step/whole-step approach to the note of resolution. The last example uses mostly chromatically altered pitches that are not diatonic, resulting in half-step approach to the note of resolution from above and below that note. A general rule, then, is that increased chromaticism will normally result in an increased level of dissonance.

How to Practice Changing Tones

Use the example on the previous page as a model for practicing changing tone figures. Learn the preceding three patterns[27] and play them over the ii-V-I progression in every key. After this is accomplished, start applying these figures to real music by playing changing tone figures of varying dissonance levels over each successive chord in the piece being studied. This is difficult and tedious work, but the rewards are well worth the effort.

3.6 The Octatonic (or Diminished) Scale

There is another eight-note scale that is very popular in jazz improvisation and it is called the octatonic scale (also known as the diminished scale).[28] The pattern in its construction is very simple: it is made up of a series of alternating whole-steps and half-steps. Here is the octatonic scale starting on C:

Octatonic Scale starting on C

Now, we will transpose it twice—each time a minor second up, to determine the octatonic scale built on C♯ and D. (Enharmonic spellings are used whenever convenient.)

Octatonic Scale starting on C♯

Perform the same operation once more (to determine the octatonic scale starting on E♭):

Octatonic Scale starting on E♭

Figure 30

Compare the octatonic scale starting on C with the octatonic scale starting on E♭. What is the relationship between the two? The two are identical (ignore enharmonic spellings). This scale duplicates itself when transposed at the interval of a minor third. Is the same true for any other scales you may know? This occurs with the whole tone scale as well. Otherwise, it is quite rare owing to the fact that most scales do not have such regularly occurring intervals between their pitches, and thus do not duplicate themselves through transposition. Why does this occur with this scale? This phenomenon has a rather delightful consequence for the improviser—it means that there are only three different octatonic scales (shown in the first three examples in this section). The scale on C is identical to the scale starting on E♭, F♯, and A. The scale starting on C♯ is identical to the scale starting on E, G, and B♭. And lastly, the scale starting on D is identical to the scale starting on F, A♭, and B.[29]

Applications

There is an interesting facet to this scale that has a great deal to do with its tonal function and its application in jazz improvisation. First, we will build two chords using the pitches in this scale. In the following example, using the octatonic scale on C, the odd-numbered pitches have been assigned to the first chord (F♯°7), and the even-numbered pitches to the second chord (G♯°7).

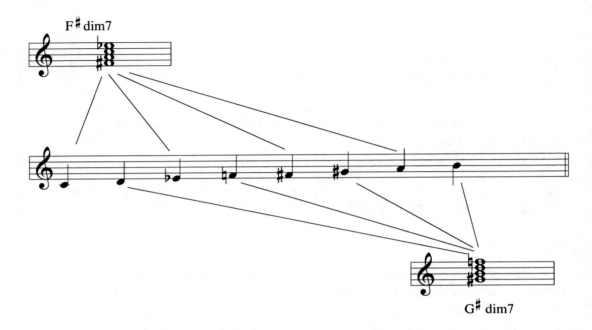

Figure 31

As shown above, the scale itself contains *two fully diminished seventh chords* whose roots are one whole tone apart. This feature of this scale makes it particularly useful for playing over fully diminished seventh chords, and in fact, this is one of the most common ways in which it is used by jazz musicians.

There is another application of the octatonic scale, one that is closely linked to its use with diminished seventh chords. The diminished seventh chord (built on $\hat{7}$) functions in much the same way as the dominant seventh chord (built on $\hat{5}$). In fact, their harmonic functions are so similar, they are virtually interchangeable. We will now examine them briefly to determine their relationship. The entire chord below is G7, ♭9 (V7 in C).

Figure 32

Notice that B°7 (vii°7 in C) is contained within G7, ♭9 (the four notes in the treble clef are B°7). The two are identical except for one pitch, G. Thus, the octatonic scale, so well-suited for diminished seventh chords, is also useful in conjunction with dominant seventh chords. If we play this scale over a dominant seventh chord, it colors the improvisation by sounding some very dissonant, yet desirable, upper structure pitches.

Play the following example which uses an octatonic scale over the dominant seventh chord.

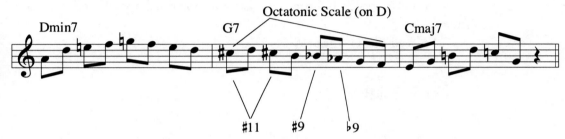

Thus, the use of the octatonic scale (beginning on the lowered ninth of the dominant chord in question) provides both primary chord members (Root, 3rd, 5th, 7th) and the colorful altered upper structure pitches, and, perhaps most importantly, the dissonant altered pitches resolve by step into the consonant primary chord members. Use of the octatonic scale in this manner provides the improvisation with much-needed tension and release.

Common Octatonic Patterns

Here are two common patterns that can be heard in many jazz improvisations.

i) Changing Tone Figure

and so on...

ii) Whole Tone Pattern

and so on...

Figure 34

The Ambiguity of the Diminished Seventh Chord

Each pitch in any diminished seventh chord is a minor third away from each subsequent pitch, and therefore, this chord repeats itself through transposition (at the minor third) as does the octatonic scale.[30] Thus, if we disregard enharmonic spellings, there are really only three different diminished seventh chords (each serving in a total of four different roles as four different enharmonic spellings of the same four pitch classes).

To demonstrate this phenomenon, we will build four different diminished seventh chords (whose roots are a minor third apart), and compare them.

i) F#°7 (vii°7 in G minor)

ii) A°7 (vii°7 in B♭ minor)

iii) C°7 (vii°7 in D♭ minor)

iv) D#°7 (vii°7 in E minor)

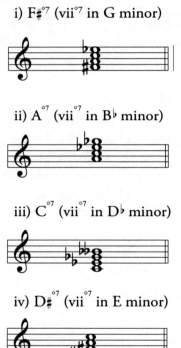

Figure 35

Compare the pitches in the preceding chords. If enharmonic spellings are taken into account, we see that they are all comprised of the same four pitches. In the same way, the diminished seventh chords built on E, G, B♭, and D♭ (one half step above the set in the preceding example) are made up of the same four pitches, as are the diminished seventh chords built on F,

A♭, C♭, and E♭♭ (one whole step above the set in the preceding example). If we continue this process of transposition by half step once more, we arrive at diminished seventh chords built on F♯, A, C, and E♭—our original set in a different order. Thus, when we take enharmonic spellings into account, there are only three distinct diminished seventh chords.

While each diminished seventh chord has a specific function in its home key, they all rely on context (key) to give them their specificity. Without tonal context, these chords are indistinguishable from one another and are therefore very ambiguous.[31]

This ambiguity is exactly the same as that which occurs with the octatonic scale. There are three octatonic scales and three diminished seventh chords—one scale for each chord. This is why the octatonic scale is most often referred to as the "diminished scale" by jazz musicians. While this sounds quite simple, it is actually much more complicated. To use the scale effectively, one must take into account the aforementioned tonal context and learn how to tailor the scale to the given key so as to highlight the appropriate pitches. In this way, one can provide direction to this very symmetrical, and thus ambiguous, scale.

Double-diminished chords

One of the more striking types of sonorities found in jazz is the so-called "double-diminished" chord. This chord utilizes all eight notes found in the octatonic scale in a particular type of vertical arrangement. This arrangement consists of taking the two diminished chords found in the octatonic scale and superimposing one on top of the other in a particular manner that is largely tertian in nature.

For the sake of example, we will use the octatonic scale starting on C. Here is the earlier example once again:

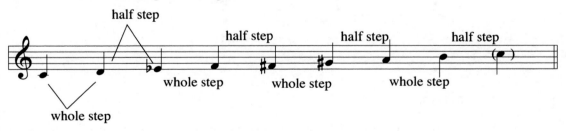

Figure 30a

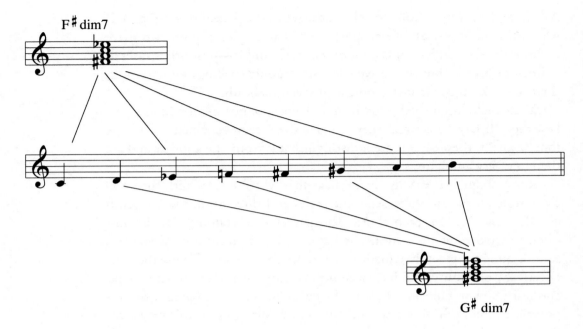

Figure 31

Notice that the roots of the two diminished seventh chords in the octatonic scale are a whole tone apart from one another.

In the middle register of the piano, play the lower chord (in this case F#^{o7}) in your left hand, and the higher chord (G#^{o7}) in your right hand as shown below:

Double-diminished chord

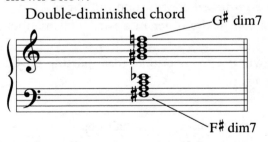

Figure 36

Again, note that this eight note chord uses all the pitches in the octatonic scale. While interesting and enigmatic on its own, this chord is used most often as an upper structure extension on the dominant seventh.

To demonstrate this usage, place a bass pitch D under the double diminished seventh chord:[32]

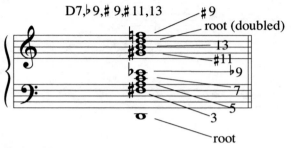

Figure 37

By placing a bass pitch under the double-diminished chord (one that is closely related to the diminished seventh chord in the left hand), the upper structure nature of this dense chord is brought into tonal focus as a very extended tertian chord based on D7. In this case (as shown in the previous example), the resultant chord when viewed as tertian is D7, ♭9, ♯9, ♯11, 13. Thus, what we have here is really just another category of upper structure polychords—one that provides a relatively simple way of constructing the towering tertian structure shown above.

3.7 Modal Improvisation

Modes[33] are simply rotations of the diatonic (major) scale. We should remember that the two scales with which we are most familiar (the major scale and the natural minor scale) are both modes. The other modes are unfamiliar because they have been used far less than the two popular modes previously mentioned. Jazz musicians have used modal writing from the very beginning (the blues in its simplest form uses several different mixolydian modes). Jazz musicians began to use the more obscure modes in a search for new sonorities in the 1950's. Jazz composition and improvisation prior to this time relied predominantly on the major and minor scale system. The introduction of these colorful "new" modes provided interesting new possibilities in the areas of improvisation and composition.

There are seven modes available using the diatonic scale. Each has its own, unique melodic and harmonic characteristics, brought about by the placement of whole-steps and half-steps within each individual rotation. Each mode, then, requires its own unique name.

Modes of the Diatonic Scale

Figure 38

The modes have both tonal and modal applications.[34]

Mode	Tonal Application	Modal Application
Dorian on D	D min7	D Dorian
Phrygian on E	E7 sus, ♭9	E Phrygian
Lydian on F	F maj7, ♯11	F Lydian
Mixolydian on G	G7	G Mixolydian
Aeolian on A	A min7	A Aeolian
		(A minor)
Locrian on B	B min7, ♭5	B Locrian

The student should practice each mode on every pitch. Once accomplished, they should be applied as listed above. While at first this may seem an inordinately involved and complicated task, it is, in reality, quite manageable because of our prior familiarity with the major scale from which all the modes are derived.

3.8 The Blues Scale

The blues scale is a six-note scale that is closely linked to the pentatonic scale (discussed in detail in section 2.2). It is the same as the pentatonic scale, except that one pitch has been added—a passing tone between 4 and 5. Thus, it combines elements of both the pentatonic scale and the be-bop scale.

Blues Scale (on C)

Figure 39

The blues scale is an essential part of jazz grammar. It works very well in blues forms (on any chord in the form), and in rhythm changes (in the 'A' section especially). It works equally as well if quoted briefly in other non-blues related forms. There is one caveat however. Because of its ability to fit over so many chords without there being any noticeably "wrong" pitches, it has become a favorite of rock musicians, folk musicians, and other musicians in the popular music genre. Thus, the jazz musician must be very careful not to overuse this simple scale. If overused, it quickly becomes monotonous and the resultant improvisation can easily become a cliché.

3.9 The Whole Tone Scale

The Whole Tone Scale[35] is a six-note scale, another in the limited number of scales that duplicate themselves when transposed. The scale is made of successive whole-steps, and as such, there are only two whole tone scales. This makes learning the scales very easy.

Unfortunately, this easy scale has a rather limited number of uses. While most jazz musicians use the scale to some degree, it is also true that most use it sparingly, to say the least. It is most commonly associated with Thelonius Monk, whose unique and highly-personalized style was particularly suited to the harmonic and melodic peculiarities of the whole tone scale. A favorite sonority of Monk's was a dominant seventh chord with a raised fourth. In classical music, this is referred to as the French Augmented Sixth[36] chord (a linear chord[37]). It is the chord over which the whole tone scale fits best, and as such, the scale is often used in conjunction with this chord.

Whole Tone Scale on C   Whole Tone Scale on D♭[38]

Figure 40

CHAPTER 4: THE ASCENDING MELODIC MINOR SCALE

The ascending melodic minor scale can be found in jazz from the music's earliest days. It was not, however, used as a defining element until the 1950's. The scale and harmonies derived from it can be heard in the music of Bill Evans, Herbie Hancock, McCoy Tyner, John Coltrane, Wayne Shorter, Miles Davis, Horace Silver—indeed most jazz musicians utilize this scale to some degree. These artists used some of the same materials, yet achieved strikingly different results. This is a testament to the wealth of melodic and harmonic potential of the ascending melodic minor scale. Since the late 1950's (and earlier to a lesser degree), jazz musicians have relied heavily on this scale. It is therefore necessary to become intimately familiar with this important scale, its "modes," and the harmonies derived from it.

The ascending melodic minor scale (on C):

Figure 41

Now, we will build seventh chords[39] on each scale degree:

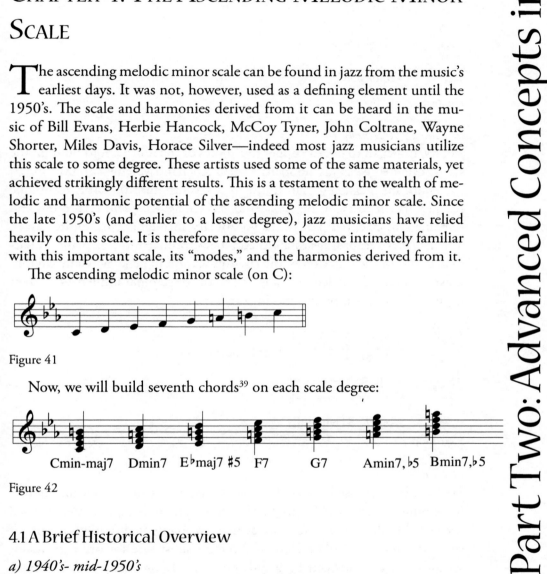

Figure 42

4.1 A Brief Historical Overview

a) 1940's- mid-1950's
The seventh chord built on the tonic is a minor chord with a major seventh. This chord can be found throughout the literature of the 1940's and 1950's in the music of Duke Ellington, Dizzy Gillespie, Charlie Parker, Horace Silver, Thelonius Monk, Tadd Dameron, Art Tatum, and others. The use of this chord as a consonant sonority increased with time until, by

Part Two: Advanced Concepts in Jazz Improvisitation

the mid-1950's, it had become a commonly found chord in jazz harmony.

Cmin-maj7

Figure 43

b) Late 1950's-Early 1960's

Bill Evans began to use the upper four notes of the ninth chord built on the sixth scale degree as his standard *rootless* left hand voicing for any "min7, ♭5" chord (also called a half-diminished seventh chord).[40] This technique reached its maturity on his *Sunday at the Village Vanguard* recordings and remained an essential part of his vocabulary throughout his entire career. The *Vanguard* recordings established a new approach to jazz piano in particular and to the function of the rhythm section in general. Many rhythm players today acknowledge Evans as one of *the* seminal influences in their development as composers and improvisers.

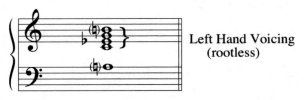

Left Hand Voicing
(rootless)

Amin7,♭5 (with 9th)

Figure 44

c) 1960's

Herbie Hancock used many of the same materials from the ascending melodic minor scale as did Evans, but his development led elsewhere. He used the chord built on the third scale degree (an augmented triad with a major seventh) and its related scale as a standard substitute for ordinary major seventh chords. This can be heard most overtly on many of the famous Miles Davis and Wayne Shorter recordings made during the 1960's.

This and other related developments account for much of the surprising and highly artistic treatment of standard and original literature found on these important recordings. It should be stressed that the ascending melodic minor scale is only one facet of Hancock's and Evans' innovations during the 1960's. Like Evans, Hancock almost single-handedly established a new direction—a new school, and like Evans, his remarkable contributions can be heard in the playing of virtually every contemporary jazz pianist.

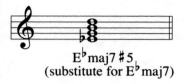

E♭maj7 ♯5
(substitute for E♭maj7)

Figure 45

d) Summary of Historical Overview

The examples above show (in a general way), the manner in which harmonies derived from the ascending melodic minor scale developed in jazz history. This development can be summarized by looking at these chords as being part of a continuum in the search for new harmonies, within a context of functional, (albeit extended), tonality. Figure 46 shows the relationship between the preceding figures in this section. In essence, they are all part of a large tertian structure whose most striking characteristic is the augmented triad contained in the center of the chord. As a rule, the augmented triad is avoided in most tonal music (including early jazz) because of its tonal ambiguity. As jazz progressed, the search for new sonorities led to the inclusion of the augmented triad as an acceptable part of a larger tertian chord as detailed here.[41]

a) Amin7,♭5

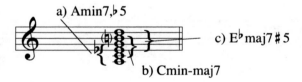

c) E♭maj7♯5

b) Cmin-maj7

4.2 The Ascending Melodic Minor Scale: Its "modes" and applications

Mode 1 (on $\hat{1}$)   Chordal Application(s):

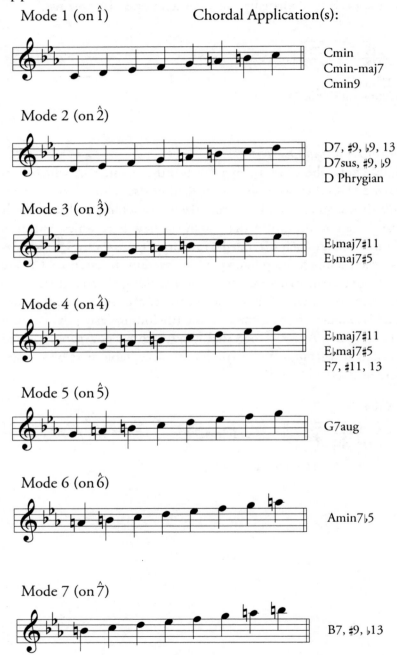

Cmin
Cmin-maj7
Cmin9

Mode 2 (on $\hat{2}$)

D7, #9, ♭9, 13
D7sus, #9, ♭9
D Phrygian

Mode 3 (on $\hat{3}$)

E♭maj7#11
E♭maj7#5

Mode 4 (on $\hat{4}$)

E♭maj7#11
E♭maj7#5
F7, #11, 13

Mode 5 (on $\hat{5}$)

G7aug

Mode 6 (on $\hat{6}$)

Amin7♭5

Mode 7 (on $\hat{7}$)

B7, #9, ♭13

Figure 47

4.3 Further Abstractions and Developments after the Hancock/Shorter/Davis Era of the 1960's

The next logical step in the development of the chord in *example c* would have been to add yet another pitch (ninth) to this tertian chord. However, the resultant chord does not present any significant new harmonic potential, hence it does not appear with any regularity in the recorded literature.

E♭maj7,9,♯5

-not found-

Figure 48

They did, however, forge ahead. Many jazz musicians like Hancock, Evans, and John Coltrane were well aware of the myriad techniques used by twentieth century composers like Stravinsky, Schoenberg, Bartok, Hindemith, Debussy, Ravel, and others (Gridley 256, 306, 309). It should come as no surprise, then, that the music became more sophisticated, more abstract, and more refined. A new technique began to emerge during this time, one that bears a close resemblance to the harmonies derived from the ascending melodic minor scale. The chord in figure 45 can also (like the previously discussed concept of polychord) be looked at as two separate layers. To be more concrete, the E♭+maj7 of figure 45 can also be conceptualized as a G major triad over an E♭ bass. What we have then, is a simple major[42] triad superimposed on top of a seemingly unrelated bass pitch. Experimentation then began with all of the possible combinations of triads and unrelated bass pitches. A new approach to jazz harmony was born, one that called for and received a new method of notation along with a new method of improvisation.

These new harmonies were notated as they had been conceptualized, that is, as a triad *over* a single pitch in the bass. The chord previously referred to as "E♭ + maj7" or "E♭ maj7, ♯5" now became "G/E♭" instead. This was preferable probably because the former was not a standard chord-type, and as such it was not easily understood or sight-read by most musicians. This type of chord became known colloquially as a "slash chord," after the slash that separates the triad and the bass pitch. (I call these circumpolar chords for reasons that will be discussed later.)

Thus, the chord built on $\hat{3}$ of the ascending melodic minor scale can be seen as a bridge between the extended tertian harmonies of earlier periods and the more advanced harmonies of today. The music of Wayne Shorter, Michael Brecker, Woody Shaw, Richie Beirach, Keith Jarrett, Dave Liebman, Peter Erskine, John Taylor, Ralph Towner, Eberhard Weber, John Abercrombie and others is saturated with these types of harmonies. However, it is in the music of Kenny Wheeler that these procedures receive, in my opinion, their most sophisticated, meticulous, and consistent treatment.

Note also that the stylistic genres represented by the aforementioned artists are extremely varied—in fact, one could say that some are diametrically opposed. This stylistic diversity occurs because of the rich harmonic and melodic potential found in these new circumpolar chords. (Discussed in section 6.6)

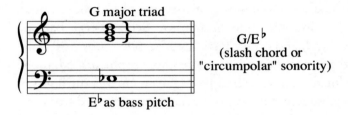

Figure 49

CHAPTER 5: THE PENTATONIC SCALE

The pentatonic scale,[43] by definition, is simply a five-note scale or "pitch collection." There are two main types of pentatonic scales, the major pentatonic scale and the minor pentatonic scale. The term "major pentatonic scale" refers to a particular five-note set of pitches consisting of $\hat{1}$, $\hat{2}$, $\hat{3}$, $\hat{5}$, and $\hat{6}$ of any major scale. The term "minor pentatonic scale" refers to a particular five-note set of pitches consisting of $\hat{1}$, $\hat{2}$, $\hat{3}$, $\hat{5}$, and $\hat{6}$ of any ascending melodic minor scale. Both have been used in jazz improvisation from its earliest days. The minor pentatonic was used primarily as a variant of the blues scale, and the major pentatonic was used sparingly in compositions whose harmony was primarily tertian. However, beginning in the late 1950's, the major pentatonic scale became increasingly more popular. The culmination of this drive can be seen in the music of McCoy Tyner, Chick Corea, Wayne Shorter, Freddie Hubbard, and others. Their application of pentatonic scales resulted once again in a move towards greater intellectual abstraction in jazz improvisation. Since this development, (which took place approximately between 1965 and 1975), pentatonic scales have become a standard tool of virtually all jazz improvisers. Today, jazz musicians use pentatonic scales in varying degrees in the following ways:

1. In pieces whose harmony is explicitly pentatonic (i.e. compositions whose harmonies are quartal, modal, or polychordal) and

2. In pieces from the standard literature, whose harmony is essentially tertian. In this case, the use of pentatonic scales results in an exciting, modern, and more dissonant interpretation of familiar standards.

Pentatonic scales have been used extensively by the younger generation of jazz musicians, who have thus been able to claim as their own an important part of the literature which had often been eschewed on the grounds that these improvisational vehicles were the voice of an older generation, and were thus not viable as honest vehicles for young musicians in the latter third of the twentieth century.

How to Practice Pentatonic Scales

Major Pentatonic Scale on 'C'   Minor Pentatonic Scale on 'C'

Scale degree: 1   2   3   5   6   1   2   3   5   6

(using C major)   (using C ascending melodic minor)

Figure 50

[Note: Major and minor pentatonic scales share four common pitches. Thus they are identical except for one pitch—or, put another way, the minor pentatonic is the same as the major pentatonic except that $\hat{3}$ is lowered by one semi-tone.]

Patterns for Learning Pentatonic Scales

Pentatonic scales are easier to use when they are arranged in groups of four, rather than five (as in the scale itself). This is due to the fact that the most popular time signatures in jazz are 4/4 and 3/4, neither of which divides by five very well. So, we will practice the pentatonic scale in groupings of four using all of its inversions. Here is the C major pentatonic scale again:

Figure 51

Now we will notate it using four-note groupings in root position and its four inversions:

Root Position   1st Inversion   2nd Inversion   3rd Inversion   4th Inversion

Figure 52

If we tried to learn this pattern in all of its inversions using scale degrees, it would become confusing—root position would be $\hat{1}\,\hat{2}\,\hat{3}\,\hat{5}$, first inversion would be $\hat{2}\,\hat{3}\,\hat{5}\,\hat{6}$, second inversion would be $\hat{3}\,\hat{5}\,\hat{6}\,\hat{8}$, and so on. The difficulty would compound when descending. Instead of using scale degrees, we will simply assign a number to each pitch in every position based on the where that pitch occurs within its inversion. Thus, the pattern shown here using scale degrees $\hat{1}\,\hat{2}\,\hat{3}\,\hat{5}$, becomes simply 1 2 3 4. The first inversion continues the pattern exactly *beginning on its own particular starting pitch*. The second inversion does the same, followed in turn by the third and fourth inversions—all repeating the numerical pattern 1 2 3 4. Here is the same example with the numerical pattern shown underneath:

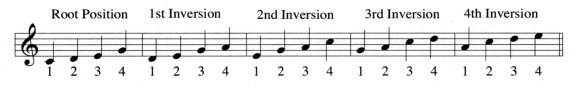

Figure 53   Numerical patterns for practicing

In this way, some very complicated patterns can be learned and easily memorized, since they are all the same numerical patterns, albeit using different inversions of the pentatonic scale.

The patterns in the following examples are notated in two different ways, the first of which uses scale degrees, which appear *above* each note. Observe that this becomes more difficult as the pattern ascends into (and past) the first octave. Now look at the method using the generic four-note numerical pattern which appears *under* each note. This method is preferable to the other method because it simplifies the more complicated scale degree pattern by viewing *all* patterns as simple four-note sequential groupings of the pentatonic scale in its various inversions. Note that the pattern does not retrograde when descending (1-2-3-4 ascending does not become 4-3-2-1 when descending). This method makes it easy to practice the pentatonic scale in all its permutations, ascending and descending, without undue strain.

First Pattern (1234) using C major pentatonic scale:

By scale degree: 1 2 3 5 2 3 5 6   3 5 6 1 5 6 1 2   6 1 2 3 and so on...

Four-note pattern: 1 2 3 4 1 2 3 4   1 2 3 4 1 2 3 4   1 2 3 4 and so on...

Figure 54

List of Numerical Patterns for Pentatonic Scales

1234 (see prior figure)	2134	3124	4123
1243 (see next figure)	2143	3142	4132
1324	2341	3241	4231
1342	2314	3214	4213
1423	2431	3412	4312
1432	2413	3421	4321[44]

Second Pattern (1243) using C major pentatonic scale

1 2 4 3 1 2 4 3   1 2 4 3 1 2 4 3   1 2 4 3 and so on...

Figure 55

5.1 The Ambiguity of Pentatonic Scales

Pentatonic scales are inherently much more tonally ambiguous than many larger collections such as the seven-note major scale. Because of this ambiguity, the pentatonic scale (especially the major pentatonic scale) allows itself to be used over a variety of different and distantly related chords as well as virtually every chord *type*.

a) C Major Pentatonic Scale can be used over the following chords:

C maj7	D min7
D7sus4	E min7
F♯ min7, ♭5	F maj 7, ♯11
B Locrian	G7, 13
E7, ♯9, ♭13	G7 sus 4
A♭ maj7, ♯5	A min 7
F min-maj7	B min7, ♭5
B♭ 7, 9, ♯11, 13	Blues in C (major key)

b) C Minor Pentatonic Scale can be used over the following chords:

C min7	C min-maj 7
C min 13	A min7, ♭5
E♭ maj7	B7, ♯9, ♭9, ♭13
F7, 13	Blues in C (minor key)
Blues in A (major and minor)	

The minor pentatonic has fewer applications because it contains a tritone between $\hat{3}$ and $\hat{6}$, which makes it much more tonally unambiguous than its major counterpart.

Of course, there will be varying degrees of dissonance in the various applications of each pentatonic over a given chord. Thus it is the responsibility of the performer to use these tools in an intelligent and musically sensitive manner. Personal taste and discretion must be allowed to dictate each person's harmonic and melodic vocabulary, so as to ensure an honest reflection of that individual's aesthetic values.

5.2 Further Abstractions with Pentatonic Scales

One of the primary concerns of all improvisers and composers (in art music) is how to achieve balance between unity and variety. Improvisers using pentatonic scales will quickly discover that these five-note collections can quickly become monotonous. Imagine for a brief moment a scale which contains only *one pitch* and how tiresome any piece using this imaginary "scale" would quickly become. Now imagine a scale containing only *two pitches* or one which contains only three *pitches*; etc. The pentatonic scale sits near the middle of the continuum from a one-pitch scale to a 12-pitch chromatic scale, with a propensity for monotony as might be expected for a five-note scale.

In a search for more variety and harmonic color, improvisers began to use pentatonic scales that were not related to the chords over which they were played. To this end, a pattern of "weaving" in and out of different pentatonic scales that were alternately "in" (closely related to the chord; consonant) and "out" (not related to the chords; dissonant) was utilized. The unity required by discerning listeners is provided by the consistent use of the same scale (pentatonic) in both circumstances, resulting in music of dramatically increased dissonance, without the tonal disorientation which often accompanies attempts at intellectual abstraction in music.

a) Consonant (C major) and dissonant (F♯ major) pentatonic scales (tri-tone between roots)

Figure 56a

b) Consonant (C major) and dissonant (D♭ major) pentatonic scales (minor second between roots)

Figure 56b

c) Consonant (E♭ major) and dissonant (D major) pentatonic scales
(major second between roots)

and so on...

Figure 56c

Piano Voicings using Pentatonic Scales

These voicings utilize both quartal and tertian elements in their construction, resulting in a timbre which is described as "open." Wind players enjoy these voicings as accompaniment in large part because their transparent and ambiguous nature creates a very spacious and uncluttered texture, which in turn provides the soloist with a sonic landscape very conducive to improvisation.

Pentatonic Voicings using C major pentatonic scale

Figure 57a

Of particular interest is the fourth inversion of the initial pentatonic chord. It features three perfect fourths followed by a major third at the top of the chord. This is sometimes called the "So What" voicing, after the famous piece from Miles Davis' *Kind of Blue*.

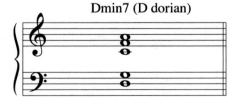

Figure 57b

The piece is probably the best known example of modal jazz and is based on only two chords, Dmin7 and E♭min7, both of which are used to signify the dorian mode (D dorian and E♭ dorian). Bill Evans used two verticalized pentatonic scales (G major and F major in fourth inversion) in his remarkably voiced response to the bass melody in the tune.

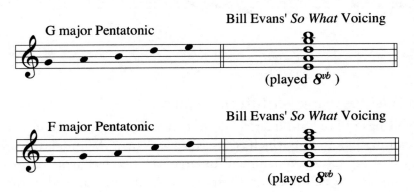

Figure 57c

Many of Evans' voicings have become the standard way to voice chords. However, his "So What" voicing has been used so often, and in so many different styles, that it is surely the most popular voicing in all of jazz piano. It is so malleable and so useful that it has been dubbed the "miracle voicing" by the legendary pianist, composer, and teacher, Frank Mantooth.[45]

A Pedagogical Note to Students and Teachers Regarding the Nomenclature of Pentatonic Scales

There is some disagreement in the jazz community when it comes to the definition and nomenclature of pentatonic scales. Many musicians, educators, and jazz theorists refer to the following set of pitches as the "C Minor Pentatonic Scale."

Figure 58

This argument rests, in part, on the assertion that a relationship similar to that which exists between E♭ major and C minor (relative major/minor) exists in pentatonic scales. Although this relationship does exist, it is peripheral, not essential in terms of definition, and leads to contradictions and inconsistencies which need to be addressed and corrected.

The analogy to the concept of relative major/minor is not valid in pentatonic scales because the context has been drastically changed by going from a seven-note scale to a five-note scale. In the seven-note major scale, each mode has a unique identity created by the changing locations of the tones and semi-tones in the various rotations (modes) of the major scale. In the seven-note context, each resultant mode or rotation of the original scale has a specific tonal identity that positively differentiates it from every other mode or rotation. The various modes are so unique, in fact, that each one warrants and receives a different name—dorian, phrygian, lydian, mixolydian, aeolian, and locrian. This however is not the case with the pentatonic scale. The rotations of the pentatonic scale do not result in five different modes. If this were the case, then each "mode" would have to be:

   i) identified in terms of structure,

   ii) unambiguously defined by demonstrating the unique harmonic implications of each rotation, and

   iii) named, using a new set of terms to identify each new "mode."

If such existed, we would expect to find some type of *ad hoc* nomenclature already in place in jazz literature or jazz theory. None can be found. No harmonies, for example, such as "E♭ major pentatonic scale—Mode 2" (used in reference to the pentatonic scale found below) actually exist in the literature.

Hypothetical Mode: "E♭ major pentatonic scale—Mode 2"

Figure 59

However, as previously noted, there are many chords over which an improviser uses this second rotation of the E♭ major pentatonic scale. These hypothetical modes do not appear because the various rotations of the pentatonic scale, although marginally different, do not present any new tonal implications that substantively differentiate any of the rotations from the original scale found in root position. What causes this phenomenon? When the context is changed from seven pitches to five, the result is that the five-note scale is robbed of the ability to rotate into discrete modes. In short, pentatonic scales lack the tonal specificity needed to invert discretely because the intervals between the five pitches are conspicuously lacking in any strong dissonance (minor second or major seventh), which means that there is neither an upper nor a lower leading tone available to assist in tonicization.

Thus, pentatonic scales are generally used as upper structure devices, and as such they exist only within the context of larger scales (implied or otherwise) which do have the ability to tonicize.

There are also pedagogical problems with the currently popular approach. First, students are told that the major pentatonic scale is made up of five pitches, $\hat{1}, \hat{2}, \hat{3}, \hat{5}$, and $\hat{6}$ of any major scale. Then they are told that the minor pentatonic is made up of five pitches consisting of $\hat{1}, \hat{3}, \hat{4}, \hat{5}$, and $\hat{7}$ of any natural minor scale. These two concepts have no unifying principle of construction in common requiring that they be identified as variants of the same "pentatonic" scale (other than the fact that they both contain five notes!) Most students (in my experience) then go through a period in which they attempt to sort out these contradictory definitions and terms for themselves. They finally manage to incorporate the inconsistent definitions into their concept of how pentatonic scales function in jazz. Then, they are told that there is yet *another* type of pentatonic scale called a "blues pentatonic" which consists of $\hat{1}, \hat{2}, \hat{3}, \hat{5}$, and $\hat{6}$ of any ascending melodic minor scale. This raises more questions that stem from the inconsistent approach and its contradictory nomenclature. This is completely unnecessary because the concept of pentatonic scales can be summarized consistently and easily from the beginning by simply giving the following definition:

> *The pentatonic scale is a five-note scale built on $\hat{1}, \hat{2}, \hat{3}, \hat{5}$, and $\hat{6}$ of any major or ascending melodic minor scale. When built using the major scale, it is called a major pentatonic scale; when built using the ascending melodic minor scale it is called a minor pentatonic scale.*

This is the method used in this text because it presents the necessary information using materials (major/minor scales) with which the student is already intimately familiar, and does so with the *least possible number of new terms* thereby providing the most consistent, logical, and concise approach to the subject.

CHAPTER 6: HEXATONIC SETS

Hexatonic Sets are simply six-note sets or "pitch collections."[46] The concept of hexatonic sets in jazz improvisation is defined as follows:
"A hexatonic set is a six-note set which consists of *any* two three-note groupings (a combination of any two major, minor, diminished, or augmented triads) that have *no common pitches*."

These six-note collections are called "sets" in order to distinguish them from scales, which have specific intervallic relationships between their constituent pitches. The use of hexatonic sets in jazz is a modern development and is featured prominently in the music of McCoy Tyner, Joey Calderazzo, Michael Brecker, Marcus Belgrave, and others.

6.1 Some Common Hexatonic Sets and their Application(s):

Hexatonic Set   Applications

1. Two major triads whose roots are one whole-step apart:

C7
C7sus
E7, #9, ♭9, ♭13
Gmin7, 11, 13
B♭maj7, #11
B♭7, 9, #11, 13

2. Two minor triads whose roots are one whole-step apart:

D7, 13
A♭7, #9, ♭9, ♭13
Amin7, 11, 13
Cmaj7, #11
B Phrygian

3. Two triads—one minor, one major—whose roots are one half-step apart:

Cmin7, 9, 13
E♭maj7, #11
D Phrygian

4. Two triads—one diminished, one major—whose roots are one half-step apart:

C7sus

5. Two triads—one augmented, one major—whose roots are one whole-step apart:

C7alt (♯9, ♭9, ♭13)
G♭7alt (♯9, ♭9, ♭13)

6. Two triads—one minor, one augmented—whose roots are one half-step apart:

Cmaj7, ♯5
A♭7, ♯9, ♭9, ♭13
D7, 9, ♯11, 13

7. Two triads—one major, one diminished—whose roots are one whole-step apart:

Cmaj7, ♯5
F♯min♭5
D7, 9, ♯11, 13
A♭7, ♯9, ♭9, ♭13

8. Two triads—both diminished—whose roots are one whole-step apart:

Cmin-maj7
Amin7♭5
F7, ♯11, 13
B7, ♯9, ♭9, ♯11

Figures 59

Patterns for Practicing Hexatonic Sets

The hexatonic set found in the first example will be used to demonstrate the patterns. The patterns illustrated will function over the following chords:

C7

E7#9, ♭9, #11, ♭13

Gmin7, 11, 13

B♭maj7, 9, #11, 13

B♭7, 9, #11, 13

The patterns following are by no means the only ones available to the improviser. Students should create more patterns as well as more hexatonic sets (there are hundreds possible).

Hexatonic Patterns:

Figure 60

6.2 Circumpolar Chords ("Slash Chords")

The concept of "slash chords" was first discussed in the closing section of 4.1. (See "Further Abstractions and Developments after the Hancock/Shorter/Davis Era of the 1960's"). To recapitulate that discussion briefly, the concept came about as a means to notate harmonies that consist of a triad over a seemingly unrelated bass pitch. Sonorities such as "E/F" (realized as an E major triad over a single 'F' in the bass) or "A/B" (A major triad over 'B') began to appear in the music of Wayne Shorter, Miles Davis, Weather Report, Steps Ahead, and a host of artists on the ECM label including Kenny Wheeler, Keith Jarrett, Ralph Towner, and Eberhard Weber to name a few. The colloquialism "slash chord" came into being as a descriptive title based on the "slash" found dividing the triad from the bass pitch. This term, while quite useful for purposes of simple identification, is of little use in explaining the musical *function* of these varied and interesting harmonies.

In order to properly name these sonorities, we need to describe the manner in which they actually function within a tonal context, for this is precisely how they do function. From careful study of many pieces written using these types of sonorities, I have observed that the bass pitch is functional while the superimposed triad acts as an *unsupported* upper structure.

This means that bass pitches generally move in tonally recognizable patterns as might be expected in pieces based on traditional tertian harmony and voice-leading principles. This type of bass motion provides the piece with a tonal foundation that is both powerful and recognizable. The triad above the bass pitch tends to function as if it were related to the bass pitch as the upper reaches of a large tertian chord built on that same bass pitch. What makes the sonority so interesting and striking is that it is missing all of the supporting pitches in between the bass pitch and its upper structure extensions. To put this another way, what we have here is a functional bass pitch with its higher-numbered tertian members (i.e. seventh, ninth, eleventh, thirteenth) without the lower-numbered members underneath. We have, if you will, a structure that is both top- and bottom- heavy, with no center. Thus, the term I suggest for these harmonies is circumpolar sonorities[47] because their harmonic information is clustered around their two "poles" without the presence of any of the expected "equatorial" pitches. In terms of balance, the functional bass pitch provides a traditional foundation which in turn makes for comprehensibility and unity, while the distantly related triad provides harmonic interest and variety by bringing a strong dissonance to the sonority.

How does this help the improviser deal with music that contains these harmonies? By viewing these sonorities in light of their two "poles," the improviser can then determine how they function within the neo-tonal context of the piece. It is possible then, through careful analysis, to determine whether the circumpolar sonority functions as a pseudo-*tonic*, *-predominant*, or *-dominant*.. One of the interesting features of these structures is that a single circumpolar sonority may function as any one of the above within the context of the piece in which it is found. The responsibility then falls on the musician to determine the function in the given context, and then proceed to tailor their improvisation accordingly.

Scale Choices and Circumpolar Chords

The following is a list of many of the most popular types of circumpolar sonorities. In each example, a C major triad is found above a different bass pitch. Included with each example are some scale choices that function well with the given sonority.[48]

1. C/B (C major triad over B)

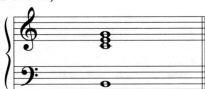

Figure 61

2. C/F

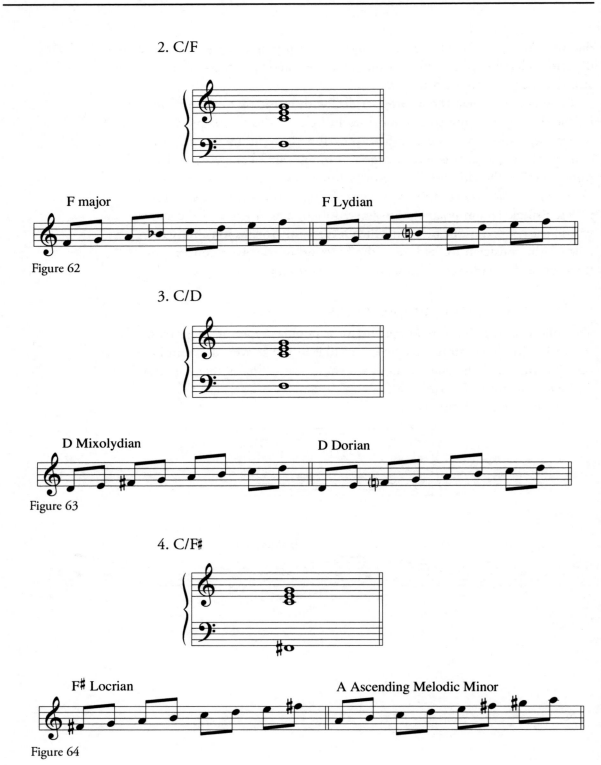

F major   F Lydian

Figure 62

3. C/D

D Mixolydian   D Dorian

Figure 63

4. C/F♯

F♯ Locrian   A Ascending Melodic Minor

Figure 64

5. C/A♭

F Ascending Melodic Minor

Figure 65

6. C/D♭

Octatonic   D♭ Ascending Melodic Minor

Figure 66

These are six of the most common types found in the literature along with some of the most consonant scale choices. This list is not complete, both in terms of possible triad/bass combinations and in terms of possible scale choices. However, it does represent the majority of types found in conjunction with this style of writing.

CHAPTER 7: REHARMONIZATION

At some point, most jazz musicians begin to write their own music—music that best suits their own unique improvisational voice. This process of becoming a jazz composer generally begins with a few intermediate steps:

1. Writing new melodies[49] for pre-existing harmonies (again, taken from jazz standards or popular songs) which is called "remelodicization," or

2. Writing new harmonies for pre-existing melodies (usually jazz standards or popular songs) which is called "reharmonization."

The first of these steps is not terribly difficult. One's ears are probably the best guide in this endeavor. The strength of the underlying chord progression will give a solid underpinning to the new melody, and therefore the result is usually quite satisfying and convincing, if not entirely original.

The second step is much more involved. Reharmonization is much more difficult because it requires much more voice-leading. One must take into account at least three voices—bass, alto (middle or inner voice), and the pre-existent melody. All three (or possibly four if a second inner voice is added) must be handled with care, intelligence, and sensitivity if the reharmonization is to be successful. [50]

7.1 An Introduction to Tonal Relationships from a Linear Perspective

To begin, we will look at the most powerful progression in tonal music—the dominant-tonic relationship from a more linear perspective, one that highlights the voice-leading, rather than the root movement.

a) In three voices only:

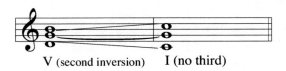

V (second inversion)   I (no third)

Figure 67

Notice that, while showing the root of the dominant as being sustained, the movement from dominant to tonic is entirely stepwise and in contrary motion; the leading tone moves to the tonic as does the supertonic.

b) In four voices:

Figure 68

The addition of a fourth voice increases the stepwise motion and results in a tonic chord that is now complete. The seventh of the dominant moves down by step into the third of the tonic chord. Of course, in jazz, it is fairly rare to find a simple triad without a seventh present.

c) In four voices (jazz version):

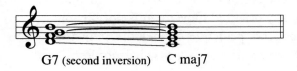

Figure 69

The jazz version of this progression includes a seventh on the tonic chord as a consonant member of the chord.[51]

Seen from this point of view, the movement from tonic to dominant and back is really, linearly speaking, as a series of three neighbor tones— one lower neighbor tone, and two upper neighbor tones as the following two examples will show:

a) Tonic-dominant-tonic as melodically-derived neighbor tones

Figure 70

Not so coincidentally, the same is true for the chord that is second in importance only to the dominant, the subdominant.

b) Tonic-subdominant-tonic as melodically-derived neighbor tones

Figure 71

From a linear or melodic perspective then, the two most important harmonies found in tonal music are both born of mostly stepwise neighbor motion with one voice that is oblique (retaining a common pitch). This is important because as harmony becomes more sophisticated, it tends to follow linear or melodic movement rather than lead it. In this way, we can see that this is true to a large degree even in simple harmonies such as I-V-I or I-IV-I where melodic or linearly oriented movement is not obvious.

Now we will look at how this principle of melodic stepwise motion (both whole- and half-step) can create exciting new harmonies

7.2 Elementary Techniques of Chromatic Harmony

a) Secondary Dominants

If we were to find the previous example in a key other than C major, it would not alter the relationship between G7 and C maj7—they would still maintain their dominant-tonic relationship. Their relationship does not change because the key has changed; only the context has changed. If we found these two chords in the key of G major, G7 would obviously not be the dominant seventh chord (in G major D7 is the dominant seventh). When this chord is encountered in the key of G major, it is known as a secondary dominant.[52] This is due the fact that it is a dominant-type chord that is not the primary dominant in the key (that being D7 in this case). However, there is still dominant-tonic relationship and function, only it is not with the actual tonic and dominant of the key.

Secondary dominant (with roman numerals):

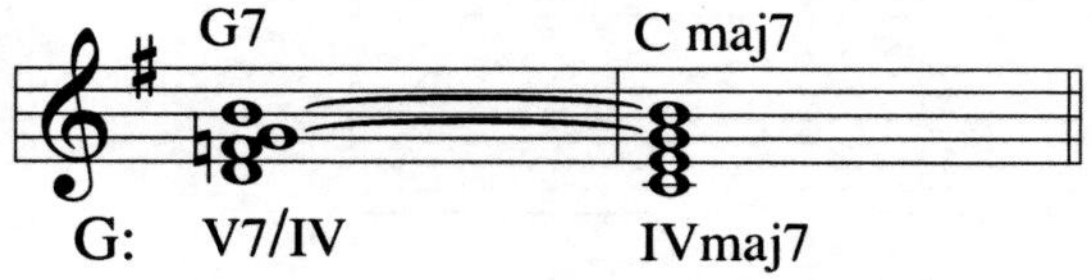

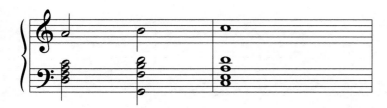

Figure 72

As shown, the roman numeral analysis for this would be: "V7/IV (read as "five-seven of four"). This shows the dominant role being played by G7, which is secondary to the primary dominant in the key, D7.

The introduction of secondary dominants is one of the simplest means to reharmonize melodies. The use of secondary dominants introduces pitches from outside of the main key, which makes for more colorful and interesting harmony than would otherwise be possible.

b) Secondary Dominants in reharmonizations of ii-V-I

Here is a short melodic fragment whose underlying chord progression is a simple ii-V-I:[53]

Figure 73

Now we will reharmonize the melody using a secondary dominant instead of ii min7 (supertonic). To do this, we must first pretend that the chord following our intended secondary dominant is itself a "tonic," if only for an instant. Thus, if G is our temporary "tonic" we can easily determine that D7 would be suitable as a secondary dominant because it is the primary dominant in the key of G major. Here is the same melody with a secondary dominant V7/V instead of ii min7:

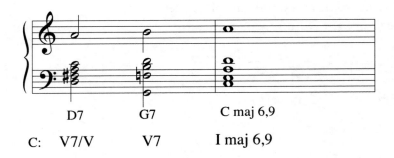

Figure 74

Notice how much more colorful the second version is with the addition of a secondary dominant. This is not to say that this substitution is always preferable—it may not be desirable. However, it is a simple and colorful manner in which to brighten up an otherwise diatonic progression.

There are some limitations, however. For example, if the melody note conflicts with the proposed altered pitch, then the secondary dominant may not be possible (F♮ vs. F♯ in this example).

Examine the following melody which has been altered to reflect this situation:

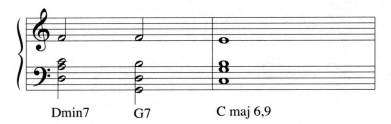

Figure 75

In this instance, the insertion of the same secondary dominant (V7/V) would create a fairly strong dissonance with the melody as shown in the following example:

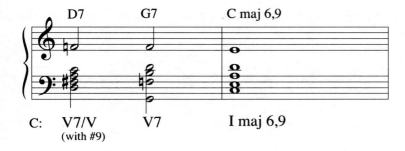

Figure 76

While this is quite dissonant, it might be entirely acceptable. Remember that jazz harmony is chromatic and uses all twelve pitches freely. Thus, the inclusion of a raised ninth is not really surprising at all. The decision here would depend on whether the use of this more dissonant chord member would enhance or disturb the melody note, which in turn may depend on the instrumentation or other factors. For example, if this melody where to be played by a professional tenor saxophonist or vocalist, the inclusion of the secondary dominant would not cause any distress—the professional would instantly hear the alteration and know that his or her melody note "changed" from the third of the chord to the raised ninth; however, if the saxophonist or vocalist is inexperienced, this secondary dominant alteration might be too difficult because of the dissonance involved in the raised ninth. Thus, as always, melodic and contextual considerations are of utmost importance in matters of reharmonization and chord substitution.

c) Strings of Secondary Dominants

This process of adding secondary dominants can continue for quite some time, resulting in a string of secondary dominants and some very lovely new harmony. Consider the following short progression and its melody:

Figure 77

It should be somewhat familiar. Here it is with a string of secondary dominants (complete with many upper extensions added) from an earlier example:

F: V7/vi   V7/ii   V7/V   V7 (4---------3)   Imaj13
     A7, 13   D7,♯9, 13   G7, 13   C7sus,9,13   C7♭9,♯11, 13   Fmaj13

Figure 78

In the previous example, the string of secondary dominants begins three chords before the dominant (C7). Each secondary dominant is preceded by its own secondary dominant. Note also that in this short example, we have used eleven of the twelve available pitches (G♯ being the only one not used). This demonstrates how quickly the use of secondary dominants can change a bland diatonic melody and harmony (consisting of only seven pitches) into an exciting and vibrant landscape full of chromatic inflection and inner voice movement.

There are two more chords that also function as secondary dominants. They are the diminished triad (vii°⁶) and the fully diminished seventh chord (vii°⁷). These two chords are both dominant function chords, so it should not be surprising that they are both capable of secondary dominant activity. In the key of C major, they are as follows:

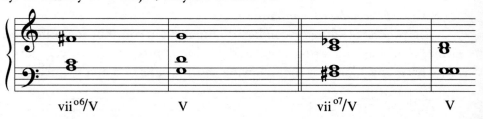

vii°⁶/V   V   vii°⁷/V   V

Figure 79

Note that each of these relies on the leading tone of the dominant (F♯). With any of these secondary dominants, it is this chromatically altered half-step approach that makes the secondary dominant such a powerful device.

Experiment with this idea by altering pieces using secondary dominants. There are countless opportunities for this type of alteration both in jazz standards and popular music.

b) Mode Mixture (or Borrowed Chords)

As discussed previously, a stepwise approach from a half-step below a given chord (most often the dominant), leads to secondary dominant harmony. However, the dominant can be approached by half-step *from above* as well. One need not venture far from the major scale to find this—it occurs regularly in the minor key.

In any minor key, the subdominant (iv) is a minor chord, and when it proceeds to the dominant, we find a half-step approach to $\hat{5}$ from above not below as in the secondary dominant. The following example shows this movement in the key of C minor:[54]

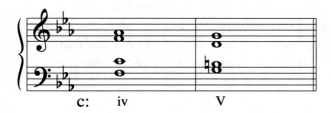

Figure 80

Here is another more famous example of the same subdominant-dominant movement, but it features the subdominant chord in first inversion, and thus the half-step approach occurs in the bass voice.

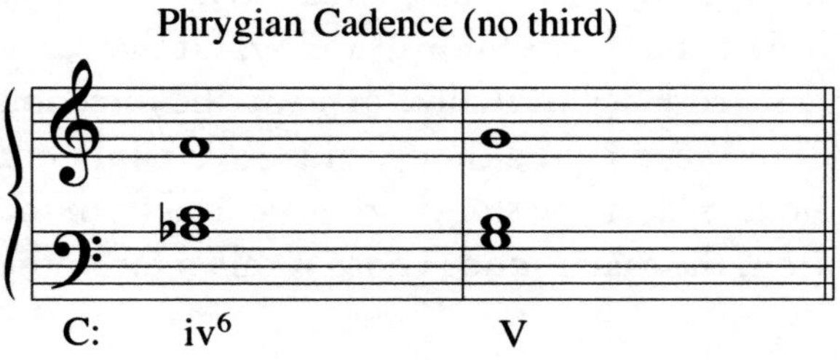

Phrygian Cadence (no third)

C: iv⁶   V

Figure 81

When found at the end of a phrase, this formula is called a phrygian cadence.[55] The term comes from the use of this cadence in the modal music of medieval period. In particular, it is the phrygian mode which is at the fore in this cadential formula.

Thus, in a minor key, the subdominant is a minor chord; in a major key it is a major chord. However, there are many instances in which the minor subdominant can be used in a major key with great musical effect. When a minor subdominant is found in a major key, it is called "mode mixture"[56] because the minor key (aeolian mode) is being "mixed" with the major key (ionian mode). This is really a function, once again, of voice-leading. As demonstrated earlier, the approach to the dominant from subdominant in a major key features whole-step approach from above and below. The approach in the minor key is by half-step from above, whole-step from below. When this half-step approach is found in the major key, a minor subdominant is created. In terms of scale degrees, it is the motion of $\flat\hat{6}$ moving to $\hat{5}$ that is responsible for this mode mixture. [57]

The minor subdominant is not the only chord that can be created using $\flat\hat{6}$. In fact there are several more chords that are used in mode mixture, most of which rely on this half-step approach to $\hat{5}$.

There are several other mode mixture chords besides the minor subdominant. Here is the complete list of commonly used borrowed chords as found in C major:

C: ii∅7   vii o7   ♭VI   i   ♭III

Figure 82

Note that most (the first four) feature $\flat\hat{6}$ as the altered pitch, while half (the last three) use $\flat\hat{3}$, and the last chord uses both $\flat\hat{3}$ and $\flat\hat{7}$. Of these, the altered pitch with the strongest tendency to resolve in a specific direction is $\flat\hat{6}$. The tendency for $\flat\hat{6}$ is to move to $\hat{5}$, although this is certainly not required. Experiment with mode mixture by substituting a chord from the minor mode where a chord from the major mode chord is called for in the following manner:[58]

   i) a minor subdominant (iv) for a major subdominant (IV),

   ii) a half-diminished supertonic (ii$^{\emptyset7}$) for a minor seventh (ii min7),

iii) a fully diminished seventh (vii°⁷) for a dominant seventh (V7),

iv) a major lowered submediant (♭VI) for a minor submediant (vi),

v) a minor tonic (i) for a major tonic (I), and

vi) a major mediant (♭III) for a minor mediant (iii).

These substitutions are not always possible. Generally, if the melody note is $\hat{6}$, the inclusion of ♭$\hat{6}$ will not be possible. Experimentation with mode mixture will result in many interesting and pleasing alterations to a wide variety of jazz standards and popular music.

c) The Augmented Sixth Chord[59] and the "Tritone Sub"

One of the most written about sonorities in classical music is the augmented sixth chord. The augmented sixth chord is not viewed as a "chord" in classical music theory. It is really more of a result of very chromatic voices moving vertically towards the dominant. We will now briefly look at how this chord is a logical outgrowth of the two reharmonization techniques just discussed—that is, we will show how the augmented sixth chord is really a combination of secondary dominant and mode mixture voice-leadings.

In classical music, the augmented sixth "chord"[60] is found most often approaching the dominant, and thus we will begin our discussion with this in mind. In order to see the genesis of the augmented sixth, we will look at three approaches to the dominant, using only three voices. The first is completely diatonic, the second features a secondary dominant, and the third uses mode mixture.

i) IV⁶-V

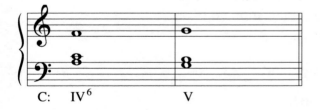

C: IV⁶   V

Figure 83

The important motion here is in the outer voices. Note that they move in contrary motion into $\hat{5}$ and they do so by whole-step in this completely diatonic version.

ii)iv⁶-V

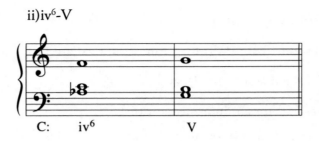

C: iv⁶   V

Figure 84

In this example, the upper leading tone of $\hat{5}$ is introduced resulting in a *half-step approach to $\hat{5}$ in the bass*, while the soprano approach is by whole-step.

iii)vii°⁶/V-V

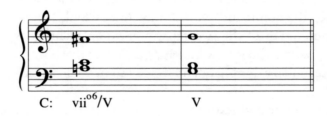

C: vii°⁶/V   V

Figure 85

In this example, the leading tone of $\hat{5}$ is introduced resulting in a *half-step approach to $\hat{5}$ in the soprano*, while the bass approach is by whole-step.

In all of the above, each chord is a recognizable diatonic triad. Rightly or wrongly then, they are all labeled with roman numerals, even though they come into being because of voice-leading.

So far, we have seen a combination of:

i) whole-step/whole-step,

ii) whole-step/half-step, and

iii) half-step/whole-step.

The augmented sixth chord is the logical next step—half-step approach in *both* soprano and bass, as shown in the following figure.

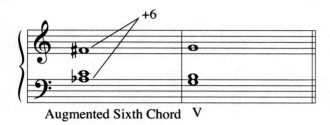

Augmented Sixth Chord   V

Figure 86

The chord gets its name from the interval between the bass and soprano. It is the result of the outer voices moving in contrary motion to $\hat{5}$. The resultant "chord" is therefore called a voice-leading chord. It cannot be found in any key because there is no key with both A♭ and F♯ in it. The following chart summarizes the increasingly chromatic voice-leading that results in the augmented sixth chord:

increasing chromaticism

C: IV⁶   V   iv⁶   V   vii°⁶/V   V   +6   V

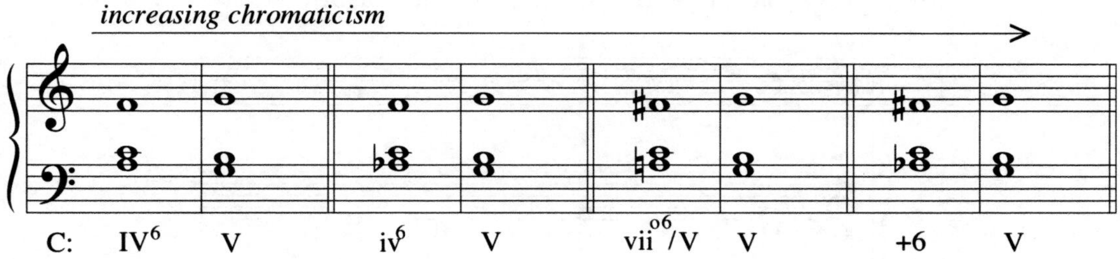

Figure 87

Some readers may challenge this last statement, and with good cause. If we consider that the F♯ in the augmented sixth chord is the enharmonic equivalent of G♭, the chord then becomes something quite recognizable— namely, it is A♭7 which is the dominant seventh of D♭. The enharmonic spelling[61] provides an interesting modulatory opportunity, and classical composers have made good use of this ambiguity to imbue their pieces with surprising twists and turns. The following figure shows two possibilities for the resolution of the augmented sixth chord in C major, one that moves more predictably to the dominant, the other capitalizing on the enharmonic spelling and modulating to the far-removed key of D♭!

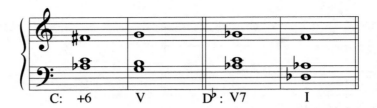

Figure 88

The preceding is a brief overview of this sonority from the classical perspective. The jazz perspective is quite different. First, we will discuss the bass movement from A♭ to G. Jazz musicians have long been aware of the fact that an appoggiatura in the bass can be easily introduced as a substitute for the proscribed bass pitch. To illustrate, let's look at the movement from ii-V in C major and some possible substitutions for the ii chord. Here is a ii-V progression in C major with a simple melody:

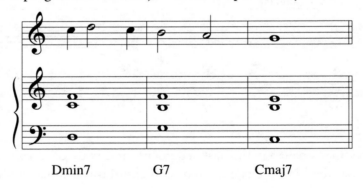

Dmin7   G7   Cmaj7

Figure 89

Here is the same example with appoggiatura movement in the bass as it moves to the dominant. The bass leaps into a dissonance (A♭) which is resolved by step into the root of the dominant (G) making for a textbook definition of an appoggiatura. While this is obviously linearly-derived, it also makes sense vertically. When the bass moves to A♭, the vertical description of the chord is no longer Dmin7; rather, it now has a diminished

5th, which means it is Dmin7♭5. This type of "substitution" (in this case introducing mode mixture to the diatonic progression) occurs frequently in jazz. Bassists regularly make this type of alteration in their bass lines and pianists react to it in their chord voicings. The only caveat here is that it must be done with the melody in mind, and some of these type of substitutions will clash with the melody, in which case another type of substitution may be a better choice.[62]

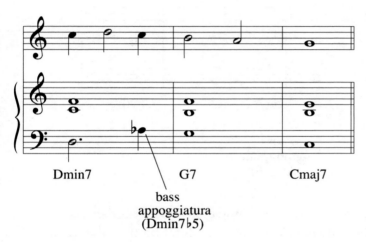

Figure 90

Now let's look at another possible substitution for our melody. In this example, the leading-tone of the dominant is introduced, and a secondary dominant is created, namely V7/V. This would be another possible substitution on its own. Keep in mind that, although we verticalize this chord and call it D7, it is really a linear phenomenon. It is a result of the third (F) becoming an F♯ which chromaticizes the movement to the dominant.

When the bassist moves to the A♭ appoggiatura, the resultant verticality again changes. As you can see, the resultant "chord" is an augmented sixth chord.

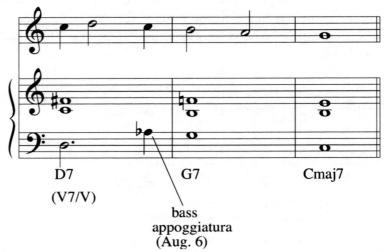

D7
(V7/V)

G7

Cmaj7

bass
appoggiatura
(Aug. 6)

Figure 91

These appoggiaturas are often found as shown here—they occur on weak parts of the beat and are much shorter in duration than the standard bass pitch. However, players often enjoy the color and variety introduced by the appoggiatura, so much so that the original chord can be dispensed with altogether and the substitution takes over as the new "standard" chord.

In this instance, the new progression would look like this:

A♭7   G7   Cmaj7

Figure 92

When the augmented sixth chord is used by jazz musicians, it is notated without the telltale augmented six interval. The preference is to use the enharmonic spelling (minor seventh) in order to make it easy to notate as a "normal" dominant seventh chord. All are familiar with A♭7, and can spell it and play over it instantly, and so this is used instead of the classical terminology. Thus, the preceding figure, it is notated as A♭7 which is known to all as the dominant of D♭.

Jazz musicians do recognize the peculiarity of this chord and they have come up with their own explanation and their own term for it. In jazz terms, it is called a tritone substitution, or the "tritone sub" (to use the colloquial short-form).

The name comes from the relationship between the roots of the primary chord and the substitution, which is a diminished-fifth or augmented fourth. Both of these intervals are made up of three whole-steps, which is then simply referred to as a tritone.[63] While this works well regardless of the chord type being substituted, it works best when the primary chord is a major-minor seventh (dominant) chord, and it is this type of substitution that is most often referred to when jazz musicians speak of the tritone sub.

The reason for this is another interesting feature of relationship between two dominant seventh chords whose roots are a tritone apart—their thirds and sevenths are (enharmonically) the same two pitches.

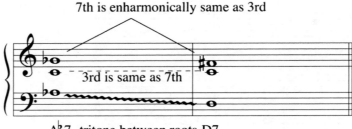

7th is enharmonically same as 3rd

3rd is same as 7th

A♭7   tritone between roots   D7

Figure 93

This is because the interval between the third and seventh of any dominant chord is itself a tritone. Recall that a tritone is a dyad of limited transposition, which means that, enharmonically, there are only six unique pairs of tritones available. Since there are twelve dominant chords, it means that each one of our six pairs of tritones are functioning as the third-seventh/seventh-third in two different dominant-seventh chords. From our earlier study of the octatonic scale and diminished seventh chords, this tritone relationship, while interesting, should not be surprising. In fact, the tritone, with its marked tonal instability, has been a source of fascination for theorists, composers, musicologists, and performers alike for many centuries.

Reharmonization Using Secondary Dominants and Tritone Substitution

These two techniques provide a large number of possible reharmonizations. Even the simplest chord progression can be refreshed in surprising ways. The following short figure will help demonstrate how this can work using very simple progressions that are mostly diatonic.

EMIN7   AMIN7   DMIN7   G7   CMAJ7

Figure 94

This short melody is shown as it would be found in typical leadsheet fashion. Harmonically, it is entirely diatonic—the chords are all found in C major—and the progression is very basic—iii-vi-ii-V-I. Note that none of the upper extensions are shown in the chord changes.

A simple harmonization of this melody, as directed by the leadsheet would resemble the following:

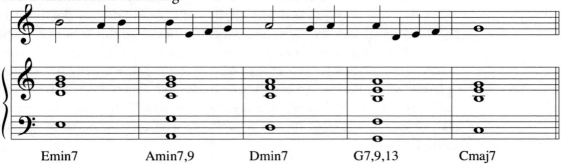

Figure 95

Note the addition of higher-numbered chord tones not indicated in the simple leadsheet. This adds a bit of color to the progression, but it would not constitute reharmonization.

Now we will add our first reharmonization. Is there anywhere that we could add a secondary dominant? The second measure seems a good place to start. A secondary dominant here would balance the harmonies nicely—we would then have a minor seventh (iii) followed by a secondary dominant (V/ii), followed by a minor seventh (ii) and another dominant chord (V). So, we will alter the second chord and make it a secondary dominant—namely V/ii.

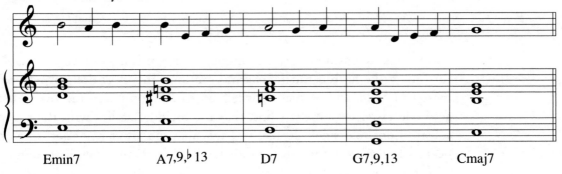

Figure 96

Note that we have also included the lowered thirteenth in this chord. This was added to continue adding color to the example. Why was ♭13 (F♮) used instead of the unaltered 13 (F♯)? This was chosen because the melody has an F♮ in this measure, not an F♯. In this way the extension remains consonant with the original melody, and thus does not interfere with it. This is not to say that melodies cannot be altered in any way—they certainly can. However, one must proceed with caution so as not to destroy the integrity of the original melody. Of course, when improvising, this is less of a concern. Horn players will imply reharmonizations in their improvisations, and rhythm players are expected to react to them. Likewise, rhythm section players will utilize reharmonizations freely and expect horn players and other soloists to hear them and react accordingly. If the reharmonization is particularly extreme, then it is probably wise to inform the musicians ahead of time.

We now have two dominant chords (V/ii and V) in our example. Before we add any tritone substitutions, let's alter both of the remaining minor-seventh chords in the example by turning them into secondary dominants. In the following example, Emin7 has been replaced by E7 (V7/vi) and Dmin7 has been replaced by D7 (V7/V).

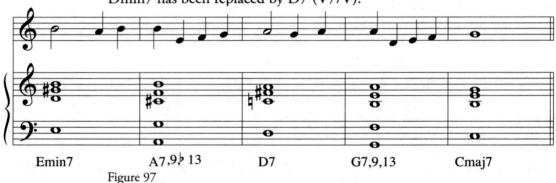

Emin7   A7,9♭13   D7   G7,9,13   Cmaj7

Figure 97

Our example is now very chromatic. In fact, this may be objectionable to some as being too much reharmonization. This is entirely a personal matter of taste, and as such it is left up to the composer and his or her aesthetic taste. Personally, I find that the melody clashes with these two substitutions to a small degree. In particular, the lower neighbor tone on beat 3 of measure 1 and 3 is the fourth of the chord and is in disagreement with the major third of the substitution. This is not a strong dissonance because, as a neighbor tone, the dissonance is mitigated to a large degree. It could easily work exactly as written in the preceding figure. However, if we objected to this dissonance, but at the same time we wanted to keep the reharmonization intact, the solution would be quite simple: alter the melody slightly to remove the dissonance between the fourth and third of these two chords.

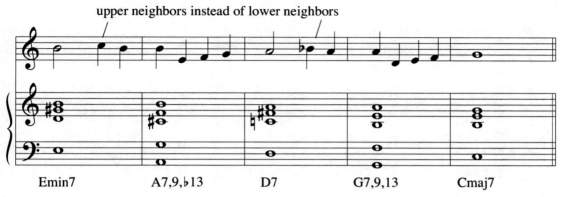

Figure 98

In this figure, the two lower neighbors have been changed to chromatic upper neighbors. These do not clash with the thirds of the chords, and are less problematic. They do, however, alter the melody, an act which may be even more objectionable to some.

We will continue with our reharmonization by using tritone substitutions. First, we will change just the dominant chord (G7) in measure 3. The tritone substitution for this chord is D♭7.

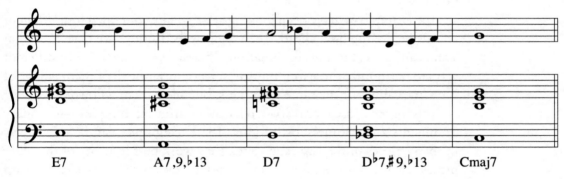

Figure 99

This creates a very smooth chromatic bass line that moves D-D♭-C in the last three measures. Note that the extensions used, namely #9, #13, agree with the melody and were chosen for that reason.

We can continue this same process with the rest of the dominant-type chords in the example. E7 becomes B♭7, A7 becomes E♭7, and D7 becomes A♭7.

Figure 100

This step makes the chords quite unrecognizable from the original. Also, note that the extensions on the chords are quite specific and require movement within two of the chords. This was done to make the reharmonization work with the given melody. The further one goes from the original chords, the more likely it is that the chords will require detailed movement in the extensions. Initially, this is done by experimentation, but with experience one can instantaneously see and "hear" which extensions will work best in a given situation.

The example we have been looking at originally contained four different chords before the final chord. The various substitutions we have looked at so far can be used in any combination. Therefore, we now have 16 different ways to harmonize these four measures. Certainly, not all of them will be of the same caliber or the same usefulness, but all of them will work.

This process used only two reharmonization techniques—secondary dominants and tritone substitutions. These techniques can be used freely in many pieces in the jazz repertoire. They work best in many of the older pieces taken from the popular music songbook (circa 1930-1955), or on those jazz standards based on these forms. They do not work as well on later repertoire (circa 1960-present) not taken from Broadway shows or popular music sources; i.e. original music actually written by jazz musicians that uses unique forms and less diatonic harmony (for example, the music of Wayne Shorter, John Coltrane, Kenny Wheeler, and others). These latter pieces are not created from the popular music templates, and thus their forms and chord changes are often unique. Altering the chords in these types of pieces, more often than not, serves to hinder rather than enhance. Their structural integrity requires the original chords to remain intact. Thus, reharmonization of this sort is not always appropriate.

Non-Functional and Linear Reharmonization

The use of secondary dominants and tritone substitutions makes our re-harmonization fully chromatic. What began as a diatonic leadsheet (using only 7 of the possible 12 pitches) quickly became a fully chromatic (using all 12 possible pitches) reharmonization, with the increase in variety and color that this implies.

Within all of this heightened chromaticism, however, the tonality of the original excerpt was maintained. This does not have to be the case; we can reharmonize and do anything we like. We can obscure the original tonality if we desire (to whatever degree we desire), or we can avoid the original tonality altogether and move to new key areas. When we reharmonize using recognizable chords, but use those chords in ways that do not function as they normally would, we call the resultant harmony "non-functional." This is not a disparaging term, even though it sounds as if it may be one. It simply refers to the fact that the harmony is not functioning according to standard tonal rules.

For example, we may find ourselves using a dominant seventh chord on G (G7). In normal tonal practice, this chord generally moves to Cmaj. In non-functional harmony, it can move literally move anywhere. From a functional viewpoint, V7 moves to I; from a non-functional viewpoint, V7 can move anywhere. In fact, the whole point of labeling it as "V7" at this point becomes meaningless, because it no longer functions as a dominant chord. This may sound as if the resultant harmonies must therefore be random, senseless, or chaotic. If not, what is holding them together? How do they work in a musically meaningful way? Our guiding principle here will be to write a new bass line with a specific melodic goal in mind, which will be the linear driving force behind our non-functional reharmonization.

There are two steps in this process:

1. Rewrite the bass line,

2. Reharmonize the chords to accommodate the *melody and the new bass line.*

This works best when the new bass line is melodically directed towards the goal chord. The new bass lines range from the simple and diatonic to the most abstract, theoretically derived bass lines imaginable. Thus, the non-functional harmonies make tonal sense because they rely on a bass line that is melodically driven.

VARIATION I: Simple Diatonic Bass Line—One Chord Per Measure (Descending)

Let's start with a simple diatonic bass line that is a relatively obvious first choice—the C major scale. There are four chords leading to our goal chord (Cmaj7), so we will begin by simply working backward from this chord, using the C major scale. The four pitches leading to C using the C major scale are G, F, E and D. Thus our first linearly derived reharmonization begins like this:

new bass line moving to the goal chord

Figure 101[64]

Once we have established our bass line, the next step is to determine the chordal options that are implied by these two lines. For this first example, we will try to keep our chords as simple as possible. To that end, we will also assume that the bass pitch is the root of whatever chord we are using. However, keep in mind that it does not have to be the root. It could be the third, fifth, or seventh of a chord. The exploration of the options presented by the various inversions may expose some wonderful harmonic possibilities, although they are too numerous for us to delve into here.

Chord 1

This chord has the melody note B (with a brief neighbor tone, C) with bass pitch G. The interval between these two pitches is a major third, which rules out any type of minor triad (assuming that G is the root). We are therefore left with two basic options: Gmaj7 or G7. Since G7 is a diatonic chord in C major, let's discard it in favor of Gmaj7, which is not diatonic and thus might be both an interesting and somewhat surprising option.

Chord 2

This chord has the melody notes B-E-F-G with bass pitch F. This one is not as apparent as the previous chord because of the number of pitches in the melody. What type of chord on F has all of these pitches in it? The E rules out a dominant seventh as well as a half-diminished seventh (both of which would have E♭ in them). The B♮ works with Fmaj7#11 and with Fmin7♭5. However, Fmin7♭5 was ruled out by the E♮, so our only remaining option here is Fmaj7#11.

Chord 3

This chord has the melody note A (with a brief neighbor tone, B) with bass pitch E. The interval between these two pitches is a perfect fourth which rules out any type of major triad, since this pitch would clash with the third of any major chord.[65] The diatonic fourth or eleventh does work with minor chords, so both Emin7 and Emin7♭5 are possible. Of these, we will choose Emin7,9,11 as our third chord.

Chord 4

This chord has the melody notes A-D-E-F with bass pitch D. This one is similar to chord 2 in terms of the number of pitches it must contain. What type of chord on D has all of these pitches in it? There is only one that con-

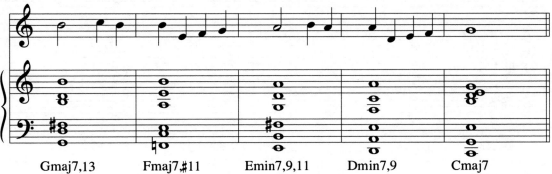

Figure 102

VARIATION II: Simple Diatonic Bass Line—Two Chords Per Measure (Ascending)

The next reharmonization features another diatonic bass line moving towards C, however the direction is altered, and thus the line approaches the goal chord from below. Also, to introduce another possibility, the harmonic activity is doubled so that we now have *two* chords per measure instead of one, as was the case in the original version. Due to this doubling of the harmonic rhythm, the bass line now requires *eight notes* instead of four and therefore starts on B.

Figure 103

The next step is to reharmonize the melody with the new bass line. As before, this was done by looking at the interval between the bass pitch and the melody note(s) and experimenting with the options available. A possible reharmonization follows:

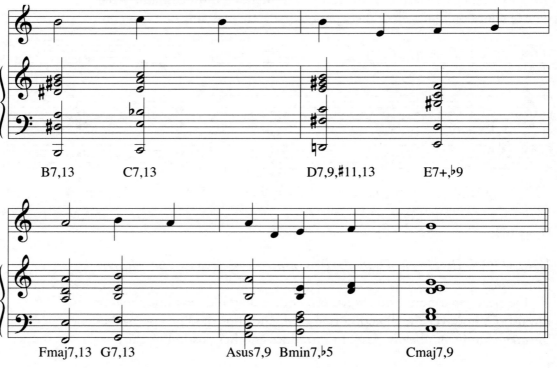

B7,13   C7,13   D7,9,♯11,13   E7+,♭9

Fmaj7,13 G7,13   Asus7,9 Bmin7,♭5   Cmaj7,9

Figure 104

This reharmonization relies heavily on dominant chords at the beginning, and these taper off towards the end because the melody is less conducive to the continuance of dominant harmonies.

VARIATION III: Diatonic Bass with Chromatic Inflection

Does the previous reharmonization work? Well, my personal opinion is that the first half is interesting, but it begins to lose focus and strength in the third measure. Thus, it might be only partially usable.

The first part of variation II did lead us to some interesting places though, and perhaps we could capitalize on that part of it and then alter the remainder of the phrase so that it fits our reharmonization. This may involve altering *the melody* in various ways as we did before.

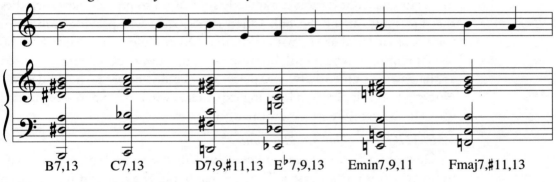

Figure 105

This example starts with the first two measures of variation II, but is altered at that point. It moves to F♯7, ♯9 and the harmonic rhythm moves back to whole note per chord instead of half note. This helps to set up a

> the original melody in the next measure which closes the
e same harmony as variation I. How did this new chord ap-
as looking for somewhere else to go after the Fmaj7 because
felt that variation II started to weaken. So, I tried F♯ as a
nst the A n in the melody. One of the options here was for a
rd on F♯ with A as the raised ninth (F♯7, ♯9). When I played
iately heard it "resolving" to Gmaj7. This setup a return of
lody and so I decided to extend the example accordingly.
d listenings, it seemed that the F♯ in this position really high-
ighted and heightened the movement to the next chord (Gmaj7), which in
turn begged for a restatement of the melody and a return home.

So, what we are really talking about here is composition. These experi-
ments in reharmonization can quickly spur us on to hearing new melodies
that are spun out of the old. Often times, they will provide wonderful
variations of familiar thematic material. Other times, the results may be
too far removed to be useful. In those cases, the new material might be used
as the basis for an entirely new piece, or it could simply be a "dead end."
Nonetheless, it is always a learning experience when we experiment in this
way, and is therefore never a waste of time.

VARIATION IV: Quartal Harmonies

Quartal harmony cannot be explained in the same way as tonal harmony which is tertian based. The problem lies in the fact that it is tonal to
some degree, and it is able to give the impression of tonal movement and
harmony, however fleating or clouded. And yet quartal harmony is also
enigmatic and ambiguous—it can imply many different harmonies and
can move freely to any of them without disorientating the listener. Quartal
harmony is most often used in conjunction with tertian harmony, in which
case its function can often be inferred from the tonal/tertian material sur-
rounding it; it can also be used homogenously which makes its tonal clas-
sification quite difficult.

To illustrate this last point, we will first harmonize a few measures from
our example using only quartal harmony. To do this, we will build our harmonies from the melody moving down from each note in perfect fourths.
We can also harmonize using diatonic fourths, which will create some augmented fourths instead of all perfect fourths.[66]

Variation IVa): Pure Quartal Harmony (*perfect fourths only*)

and so on...

Figure 106

As you can see, this type of homogenous harmony quickly becomes tiring due to its predictability. This is likely the reason that when we find quartal harmony in non-modal music, it is used sparingly and interspersed with tertian harmony. This is not to say that quartal harmony is not interesting or pleasing—the opposite is true. It is just that the sound of quartal harmony is very unique and thus, quickly identified by the listener. Note also that no chordal analysis is found underneath any of the chords. The best we could do with this is to label them all some type of suspended seventh (sus7), but this would not describe the chords as well as just saying that they are quartal.

VARIATION IVb): Diatonic Quartal Harmony

If we want to harmonize this excerpt using diatonic quartal sonorities, we have to analyze the melody to see which scales are possible. Some melodies may be possible to harmonize using more than one scale, others may be too chromatic to allow for even one scale for more than a measure or two before having to switch scales.

The melody in this excerpt is from C major, so we will build diatonic quartal sonorities using only the C major scale. Note that whenever F and B are involved, the interval is not a perfect fourth, but rather an augmented fourth.

Figure 107

Another option here would be to choose another key area for a portion of the example in order to provide a bit of variety. The first six beats could be harmonized using G major, since the F♮ does not appear until the following beat. Then, it would continue in C major as before.

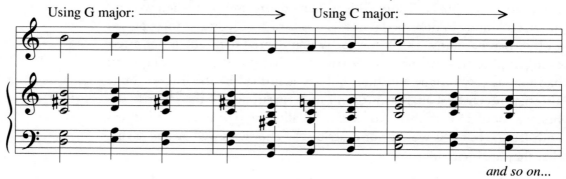

Figure 108

This example is preferable to me because the use of two different scales makes it less predictable than the previous example.

In a longer example, we could easily use more keys, as desired and a fair amount of variety can be achieved using just diatonic quartal harmony. In the following example (which uses the entire melody once again) we will access yet another key (F major) in the last two measures. Thus, approximately every six beats, our example is "losing" one sharp as we move from G major to C major and then to F major.

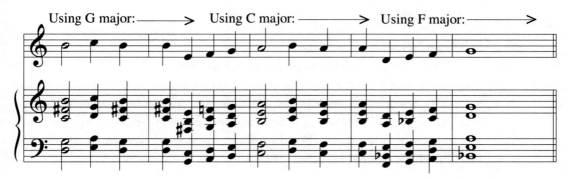

Figure 109

VARIATION V: *Pentatonic Harmony*

Closely related to the quartal harmony is a hybrid that is part quartal, and part tertian, and is made by a particular verticalization of the pentatonic scale.[67] The following reharmonization uses various transpositions of the so-call "So What" voicing, but ends on C major as in the original.[68]

Figure 110

If so desired, this voicing could have continued to the last chord. In this case, it would not have ended in C major; instead, the minor mode would have been established.

Figure 111

VARIATION VI: Slash Chords

Slash chords, like some of the other harmonies discussed, are difficult to categorize.[69] Some are dissonant (A/E♭), others are quite consonant (C/D). Some slash chords can be described using normal terminology (G/E♭=E♭major7, #5) while others cannot (C/D♭=?). Sometimes they function tonally, other times they do not. So, they are enigmatic in many ways and perhaps therein lays their charm.

Figure 112

There are no hard and fast rules in regards to the usage of slash chords in jazz. Composers seem to follow their own aesthetic voices in this as with all things, and from that comes a wide variety of music that uses slash chords. That being said, there is often a fair amount of tonal activity in the bass line itself, which often looks very similar to those found in recognizable tonal progressions. This is not always the case, but can be used as a means to organize the slash chord harmonies by providing them with specific tonal direction.

The Implications of Extended Tertian Harmony

To close this chapter, I would like to expound briefly the implications inherent when we use the large tertian chords found in jazz. Jazz is a style of music that regularly allows all of the following as normal chord members:

i)   thirds (major and minor),

ii) fifths (diminished, perfect, and augmented),

iii) sevenths (major, minor, and diminished),

iv) ninths (9, ♯9, and ♭9),

v)   elevenths (11 and ♯11), and

vi) thirteenths (13 and ♭13).

As such, any melody note can easily be altered to become any one of these pitches (and more). Consider then Figure 113 on the next page.

Keep in mind that these options are only *some* of the available for the *first* pitch in our example. Each consecutive pitch in our melody will have the same number of options, only with different chords. If we use only these fifteen options shown above as our palette of possible chords, the resultant collection is enormous. To be precise, our original melody had, coincidentally, fifteen notes in it meaning that with these fifteen options for each pitch, we would have a total of *over 430 quadrillion* (430 with 15 zeroes after it) *unique versions!* Of course, some of these are minor variations, but they are variations nonetheless.

As if this weren't remarkable enough, consider the number of options available in a real song with more than 15 melody notes. While this seems daunting, we should be happy that so many options exist for us to explore. If this were not the case, we would likely have exhausted the possible melodies and harmonies by now.

How then does one make decisions given all of these options? The only answer is to follow one's own muse and write music that is true to one's own artistic preferences. This is really the only path to artistic independence and success.

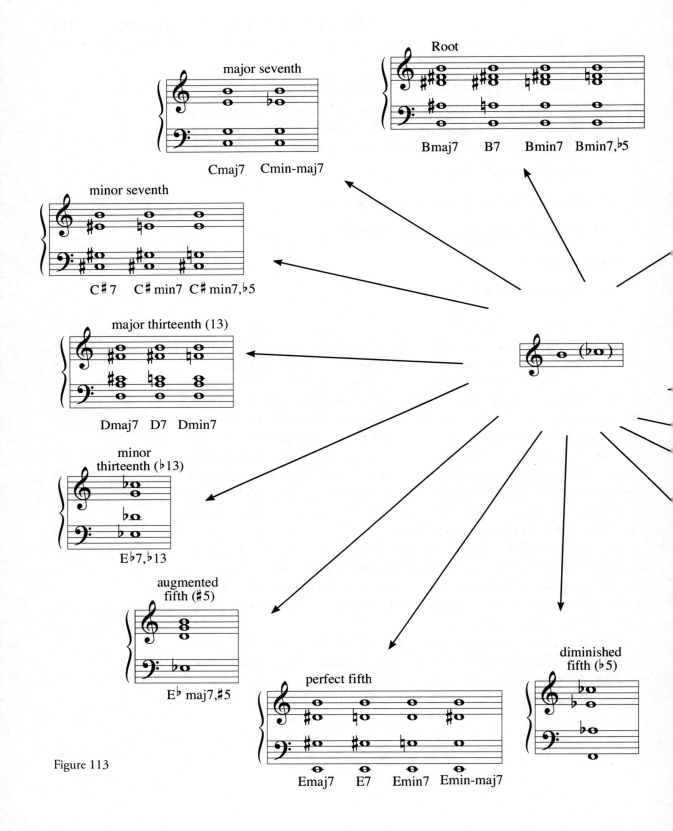

Figure 113

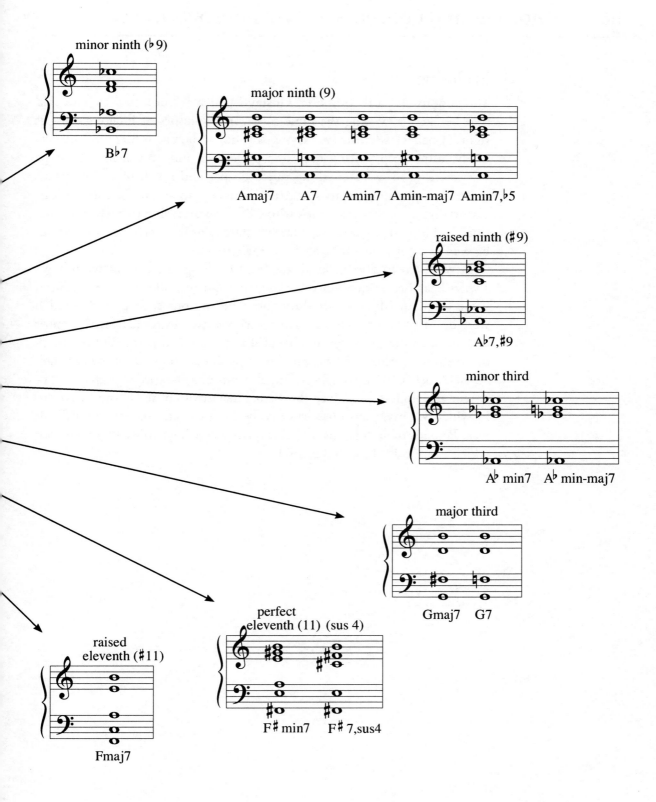

In Closing

The famous classical composer, Gustav Mahler, is purported to have said that he "kept rewriting the same piece, in the hopes of finally getting it right." I believe what he was saying was not to be taken literally—he certainly didn't keep writing the same piece over and over again. What he was referring to was something much deeper and much more important for anyone pursuing an artistic goal; that is, for an artist, the core "vision" essentially never changes. One's whole life is spent trying to perfect that vision, and in that larger sense, Mahler's statement is correct: one's work can be seen as a constant variation on a single theme.

If we listen to Stravinsky throughout his long and productive life, we always hear his unique voice coming through regardless of the medium; if we listen to Miles Davis throughout his various style periods (which were decidedly more eclectic than most), we can always identify his spirit and voice shining through unabated. In my mind, this is really the mark of greatness, without the distractions of technical prowess or stylistic fad. Artists must strive to somehow find a means of self-expression that is consistent and honest. Yet, given the virtual maelstrom of styles and situations in which we may find ourselves involved, this is an exceedingly difficult task. Perhaps then, it is this ineffable quality which we must all pursue, but which cannot, in the end, be taught.

Works Cited

Aldwell, Edward and Carl Schachter. *Harmony and Voice Leading.* New York: Harcourt, 1979.

Barzun, Jacques. Ed. *Pleasures of Music.* New York: Viking, 1951.

Beach, David, Ed. *Aspects of Schenkerian Theory.* London: Yale UP, 1983.

Benjamin, Thomas, Michael Horvit, and Robert Nelson. *Techniques and Materials of Tonal Music.* 5thed. New York: Wadsworth, 1998.

Coker, Jerry, Jimmy Casale, Gary Campbell, and Jerry Greene. *Patterns for Jazz.* Miami: Studio Publications/Recordings, 1970.

Copley, R. Evan. *Harmony: Baroque to Contemporary.* Champaign: Stipes, 1979.

Davis, Miles. *Miles: The Autobiography.* New York: Simon & Schuster, 1990.

Gauldin, Robert. *Harmonic Practice in Tonal Music.* New York: Norton, 1997.

Gridley, Mark C. *Jazz Styles.* Upper Saddle River: Prentice Hall, 1997.

Gottlieb, Robert, Ed. *Reading Jazz: A Gathering of Autobiography, Reportage, and Criticism from 1919 to Now.* New York: Random House, 1996.

Green, Douglass M. *Form in Tonal Music.* New York: Holt, Rinehart and Winston, 1979.

Hindemith, Paul. *The Craft of Musical Composition.* Book 1. New York: Schott Music Corporation, 1970.

———. *A Composer's World.* Gloucester: Harvard UP, 1969.

Jonas, Oswald. *Introduction to the Theory of Heinrich Schenker.* Trans. and ed. by John Rothgeb. New York: Longman, 1982.

Kostka, Stefan, and Dorothy Payne. *Materials and Techniques of Twentieth-Century Music.* Englewood Cliffs: Prentice Hall, 1990.

Kostka, Stefan, and Dorothy Payne. *Tonal Harmony: With an Introduction to Twentieth-Century Music* 5th ed. New York: McGraw Hill, 2004.

Lees, Gene. *Cats of Any Color* New York, New York: Oxford UP, 1995.

Levine, Mark. *The Jazz Piano Book.* Petaluma, CA: Chuck Sher, 1990.

Mantooth, Frank. *Voicings for Jazz Keyboard.* New York: Hal Leonard, 1986.

Mehegan, John. *Jazz Improvisation.* New York: Watson-Guptill, 1965.

Persichetti, Vincent. *Twentieth Century-Harmony.* New York: Norton, 1961.

Pettinger, Peter. *How My Heart Sings*. New Haven: Yale UP, 1998.

Piston, Walter. *Harmony*. 5th ed. Revised by Mark DeVoto. New York Norton, 1987.

Reilly, Jack. *The Harmony of Bill Evans*. Madison: Unichrome, 1993.

Roig-Francoli, Miguel. *Harmony in Context*. New York: McGraw-Hill, 2003.

Wennerstrom, Mary H. *Anthology of Twentieth-Century Music*. Englewood Cliffs: Prentice Hall, 1988.

Endnotes

1. The best, in my opinion, is *Patterns for Jazz* by Jerry Coker. [For complete publication information here and throughout the text, see the bibliography.]

2. For the pianist, I recommend *The Jazz Piano Book* by Mark Levine (available at most music stores in the United States and Canada). It is by far the most comprehensive text available on the subject and as such it is a valuable resource for any aspiring jazz pianist. Also, the four-volume set by John Mehegan entitled *Jazz Improvisation* contains valuable insights into the world of jazz piano. I recommend the fourth volume especially for its discussion regarding left-hand voicings.

3. For further reading on harmonies derived from these and other less conventional intervals, see Copley, Chapter 15; Kostka, Chapter 3, Persichetti, Chapters 3-8; Benjamin, Chapter 8.

4. For further reading on these harmonies and their use in late 19th- and early 20th-century music, see Copley, Chapters 2, 11; Gauldin, Chapters 37-40; Benjamin, Chapter 4.

5. For further reading on the polychord in Twentieth Century music, see Copley, Chapter 18 and Benjamin, Chapter 9.

6. There is a chord type (usually labeled "alt." which is short for "altered") referred to in many jazz charts that is largely undefined, and therefore problematic for less experienced improvisers. It usually means that there are many altered members in the chord (always of the dominant type), and the arranger/composer is assuming that the pianist will determine the correct voicing to use given the context of the piece. This, however, assumes a great deal. A safe rule in dealing with these "altered" chords is to add both the raised and lowered ninths, along with a lowered thirteenth. This formula will provide an acceptable solution most, if not all, of the time.

7. In the examples that follow, you will note that some upper structure triads are in root position, while others are in either first or second inversion. Generally this is not an essential matter—rules of voice-leading will often dictate the inversion of the upper structure. As such, the examples given are out of context (no voice-leading occurs in isolated chords) and the inversions used were chosen on the basis of sound quality more than anything else.

8. If you are unfamiliar with the concept of four-part chorale-style writing, see Copley,

Chapters 14-16; Gauldin, Chapter 6; Benjamin, Chapters 3-13. Also, for an interesting discussion of Bill Evans' approach to four-part writing in jazz, see Jack Reilly's *The Harmony of Bill Evans,* pages 16-23.

9. Many teachers and performers discourage students from notating what they have transcribed. I advocate the opposite for the following reason: First, it must be noted that, in both instances, the student acquires substantial aural skills. However, when notation takes place, so does a higher level of conceptualization—that is, the student must determine the names of the pitches, as well as their exact (as far as possible) rhythmic placement. The act of notation thus requires much more thought than simply learning the solo by simple repetition. It is therefore more beneficial to the student, who receives from it a higher level of aural skills training than would otherwise be possible. There are also other benefits—the student who notates the transcription will necessarily become more adept at sight-reading and will also be better prepared to notate their own music, when that time comes.

10. There are many programs available online that perform this function. I use a shareweare program called Amadeus which is available at www.hairersoft.com and is very reasonably priced.

11. Having used the method outlined in this section with many students over many years, I can attest to its efficacy. In fact, I have often been surprised by the quality of the improvisations which have emerged from complete beginners immediately after analyzing a piece in this way.

12. Keep in mind the simple math involved here—there are only twelve different pitches and four main chord types for a total of 48 (12x4=48) possible chords. There are also twelve different major scales, yet each scale has seven chords, resulting in a total of 84 (12x7=84) seemingly different chords in the sum total of all possible diatonic seventh chords.

13. This example does not have the half-diminished seventh type in it—if it did, it (like the dominant chords) would only have one key underneath it.

14. In fact, these two key areas, when viewed from an even larger perspective (i.e. the whole song), are also closely related. This is beyond the scope of the current discussion, however. This type of approach is what makes it possible for jazz musicians (and classical musicians as well!) to memorize a seemingly impossible amount of literature. In thinking about music this way, one need not memorize countless thousands of minute details (i.e. pitches), one instead remembers key areas, cadences, formal characteristics, melodic figures—in other words conceptual information. Ideally then, the minutia tends to take care of itself.

15. While there are, of course, many variations and alterations that result in a number that is substantially larger than 48, most feature one of the four basic chord types (major seventh, minor seventh, dominant seventh, and half-diminished seventh) at their core, making the differences between them largely inconsequential, however difficult.

16. From the liner notes found in Margitza's CD entitled: Second Home (Musidisc #500722, 1995)

17. For a complete discussion of these advanced sonorities, see 6.6.

18. To say nothing of the fact that, without a considerable knowledge of grammar and syntax, the imagined poser of this question would not be able to even pose the question in the first place!

19. I have actually heard this from beginners who object to transcription on the grounds stated.

20. Tenor saxophonist Michael Brecker (renowned for his creativity and technical virtuosity) is said to have practiced all of his scales, modes, etc. using the New York city phone book as a source for random numerical combinations. For example, if the next number in the New York city phone book was "867-5321" and he was working on the Dorian mode on C♯, he would play C♯ (8), A♯ (6), B (7), G♯ (5), E (3), D♯ (2), and C♯ (1). He probably had some system for dealing with repeated numbers and zeroes that involved changing octaves or something similar.

21. These scales are not really new scales at all. They are both slight variations on the major scale, variations so popular that they require some type of specific identification—hence they have been given the descriptive (but intellectually vacuous) colloquial name "bebop scale," after the era in which they began to appear most conspicuously.

22. Whenever scale degrees are mentioned here and throughout the text, they always refer to the home scale, which is not always the same as the mode in question. For example, note that be-bop ♯2 starts on $\hat{5}$ not $\hat{1}$, as does be-bop ♯1.

23. Three other be-bop scales are theoretically possible by simply adding a passing tone between: i) $\hat{1}$ and $\hat{2}$; ii) $\hat{2}$ and $\hat{3}$; and iii) $\hat{6}$ and $\hat{7}$. While useful in certain circumstances, these types are found less often than the main types discussed above. This is due to the chromatic passing tone which tends to destabilize the tonic when found chromatically encircling pitches other than scale degree $\hat{5}$.

24. The names of the two scales are taken from their "starting" pitch. This is useful for learing the scales, but in practice, they are used freely and can "start" on any pitch.

25. For further reading on sonata form (and other forms) see Green's *Form in Tonal Music.*

26. There are many other types of non-harmonic tones in tonal music. For a complete discussion on the various types of non-harmonic tones, see Copley, Chapter 11; Gauldin, Chapter 7; Benjamin, Chapter 3.

27. While all three types are used, ♯2 appears more frequently than the other two.

28. For further reading on the octatonic scale, see Kostka, Chapter 2; Persichetti, Chapter 2; and Piston, Chapters 30-31.

29. It is possible to start the octatonic scale with a half-step instead of a whole-step (as outlined above). The function of the scale, however, is not affected. This method results in the same scale, albeit with a different starting point.

30. This occurs because of the math involved. There are twelve semitones in the octave and the operative interval in the diminished seventh chord (a minor third) is comprised

of three semitones, resulting in an even division of the octave (12÷3=4). This results in a chord that repeats itself through transposition at a minor third.

31. Classical composers have capitalized on this ambiguity by featuring these chords as enharmonic "pivot" chords which are used in modulations of the same name.

32. This works because one of the tritones contained in F#°7 (F#-C) is the third and seventh of D7. This would also work if we placed F in the bass, since the other tritone in F#°7 (A-E♭) is the third and seventh of F7. This is another example of the ambiguity of these symmetrical chords, one that is used frequently by bassist Dave Holland in the harmony of his own pieces.

33. For further reading on these and other modes, see Copley, Chapters12-13; Persichetti, Chapter 2; Piston, Chapters 30-31; Benjamin, Chapter 5.

34. Some pieces are overtly modal (Miles Davis' *So What* for example) and will state the mode over which one is to improvise explicitly. The modes can also be used in music that is of a more traditional tonal nature—meaning that, if one sees "D minor7," one can access the dorian mode on D as an optional scale choice for improvisation.

35. For further reading on the whole tone scale, see Copley, Chapters 11-12; Kostka, Chapter 3; Persichetti, Chapter 2; Piston, Chapters 30-31.

36. For further reading on augmented sixth chords, see Copley, Chapter 5; Gauldin, Chapter 29; Benjamin, Chapter 5.

37. For further reading on linear chords, see Gauldin, Chapters 16, 28, 29, 32, and 37; Benjamin, Chapter 3.

38. Both scales should be learned starting on any pitch.

39. Note: Chords that occur elsewhere as diatonic seventh chords are notated with smaller noteheads.

40. Astute readers will note that the ninth chord built on $\hat{6}$ in the key of C minor (using ascending melodic minor) is identical to the ninth chord on $\hat{2}$ in the key of G minor (using harmonic minor scale). However, since the ascending melodic minor is used much more often than the harmonic minor scale, this text traces the development of this chord in relation to the former, rather than the latter.

41. The augmented triad is found quite often in jazz and classical music when the 5th of the dominant is raised to become an augmented 5th. This pitch ($\sharp\hat{2}$) usually resolves to $\hat{3}$ which mitigates the peculiarity of the augmented triad to a considerable degree.

42. Minor (and other) triads are possible, but the majority found in actual pieces feature major triads.

43. For further reading on pentatonic scales, see Copley, Chapter 11; Kostka, Chapter 2; Persichetti, Chapter 2; Piston, Chapters 30-31.

44. Practice all patterns using all major and minor pentatonic scales.

45. See Mantooth's *Voicings for Jazz Keyboard*. Chapter 4 "Miracle Voicings"

46. The term "pitch collection" refers to any set of pitches that function, more or less, as a singular unit within a piece of music. It is probably best used in conjunction with collections that resist identification using more traditional terminology.

47. I must express my gratitude to my wife, Rebecca, for finding the perfect name for these sonorities, which she did after a short discussion of their function.

48. I am deeply indebted to David Morgan (Youngstown State University) for his thoughts on circumpolar chords and their scales.

49. Copyright law protects melodies, but does not protect harmony. It does not (rightly so in my opinion) recognize chord progressions as being "unique." Thus, it is legal to use chord changes from a piece of copyrighted music, but it is illegal to use even a short fragment of melody from the same piece. This accounts for the odd titles found in many of the "play-along" recordings—the chord changes are identical to, for example, a Charlie Parker tune, but the melody is not; the title is then slightly altered and a "new" tune that is identical to the Parker tune has been legally recorded.

50. In classical music, both of these things occur frequently as various types of "variation" procedure (i.e. passacaglia, chaconne, theme and variations, etc.)

51. The inclusion of a seventh as a completely consonant chord member as a conclusive, final sonority is peculiar to jazz. In classical music, seventh chords are found very often, but only rarely as a conclusive, final chord. This occurs in a few pieces by Scriabin and occasionally in twentieth century works, but is not generally found in literature prior to the late 19th- or early 20th Century.

52. The following is meant as a brief review of this topic. For a more detailed discussion, see Copley, Chapter 4; Gauldin, Chapters 24-25; Benjamin, Chapter 1.

53. Remember to play through all examples on the piano.

54. Note that the dominant is approached from above in the soprano voice.

55. For more on the phrygian cadence, see Copley, Chapter 18; Gauldin, Chapter 15;

Benjamin, Chapter 9 and Part 4, Chapter 5.

56. For more on mode mixture, see Copley, R. Evan. *Harmony: Baroque to Contemporary, Part Two.* Chapter 3' Gauldin, Chapter 27; Benjamin, Chapter 15.

57. Many older texts refer to a minor subdominant in a major key as a "borrowed chord" because it was seemingly "borrowed" briefly from the minor key. This term is less popular today, "mode mixture" being the preferred name.

58. As one goes down this list, it becomes more difficult to use the chord in question. This is because many melodies will easily allow for $\flat\hat{6}$, but will not allow for $\flat\hat{3}$ or $\flat\hat{7}$ as easily.

59. For further reading on augmented sixth chords, see Kostka & Payne. Chapter 23; Roig-Francoli, Miguel. *Harmony in Context.* Chapter 23.

60. Again, the term "chord" is used as a convenience since it is not a chord in the normal sense of the term.

61. In reality, G♭ and F♯ are not the same pitch. Only the piano makes it seem so because of the unique compromise it has utilized in its tuning system.

62. Jazz musicians are constantly reinterpreting pieces in this manner resulting in highly individualized versions of standard repertoire. Of course, very little of this is notated in fake books because it would make them far too detailed for their intended use.

63. In the previous figures, note that the interval between the root of the primary chord (D) was a tritone away from the appoggiatura (A♭).

64. Note that the chromatic inflections for the previous version of this melody have been removed to make it completely diatonic once again.

65. An option in the major chord category would be to use the A as a suspended fourth. This might work if it moved to a G♯ in the following measure, which in this case it does not.

66. See section 1.2 for more information on diatonic quartal sonorities.

67. See section 5.2

68. The melody has been chromaticized in m. 3 as before in order to highlight the more interesting chromatic neighbor created.

69. See section 6.2.

Lightning Source UK Ltd.
Milton Keynes UK
UKOW02f0711260314

228841UK00008B/204/P